WHSmith

Challenge

Maths

KS2: Year 4 Age 8–9
Paul Broadbent and
Peter Patilla

Hachette UK's policy is to use papers that are natural, renewable and recyclable products and made from wood grown in sustainable forests. The logging and manufacturing processes are expected to conform to the environmental regulations of the country of origin.

Orders: please contact Bookpoint Ltd, 130 Milton Park, Abingdon, Oxon OX14 4SB. Telephone: +44 (0)1235 827720. Fax: +44 (0)1235 400454. Lines are open 9.00a.m.–5.00p.m., Monday to Saturday, with a 24-hour message answering service. Visit our website at www.hoddereducation.co.uk.

© Paul Broadbent and Peter Patilla 2013
First published in 2007 exclusively for WHSmith by
Hodder Education
An Hachette UK Company
338 Euston Road
London NW1 3BH

This second edition first published in 2013 exclusively for WHSmith by Hodder Education
Teacher's tips © Matt Koster 2013
Impression number   10 9 8 7 6 5 4
Year   2018 2017 2016

All rights reserved. Apart from any use permitted under UK copyright law, no part of this publication may be reproduced or transmitted in any form or by any means, electronic or mechanical, including photocopying and recording, or held within any information storage and retrieval system, without permission in writing from the publisher or under licence from the Copyright Licensing Agency Limited. Further details of such licences (for reprographic reproduction) may be obtained from the Copyright Licensing Agency Limited, Saffron House, 6–10 Kirby Street, London EC1N 8TS.

Cover illustration by Oxford Designers and Illustrators Ltd
Illustrations by © Hodder Education
Typeset in Folio Book 14pt by DC Graphic Design Ltd
Printed in Spain

A catalogue record for this title is available from the British Library
ISBN 978 1444 188 394

Contents

Parents' notes		2
1:	Place value	4
2:	Addition facts	6
3:	Subtraction facts	8
4:	Length	10
5:	Multiplication and division facts	12
6:	2D shapes	14
Test 1		16
7:	Time	18
8:	Fractions of shapes	20
9:	Addition	22
10:	Subtraction	24
11:	Sequences and patterns	26
12:	Comparing and ordering numbers	28
Test 2		30
13:	Rounding numbers	32
14:	Weight and mass	34
15:	3D shapes	36
16:	Multiplication	38
17:	Division	40
18:	Coordinates	42
Test 3		44
19:	Decimals	46
20:	Capacity	48
21:	Fractions of amounts	50
22:	Graphs	52
23:	Money	54
24:	Angles	56
Test 4		58
Answers		60

Parents' notes

How this book can help your child

- This book has been written for children who are between 8 and 9 years old.
- It will support and improve the work they are doing at school, whichever Maths scheme they use.
- The activities in the book have been carefully written to include the content expected of children at this stage in their development.
- The activities will help prepare your child for the different types of tests that occur in schools.

Materials needed

- Pencil, coloured pencils, eraser, watch and centimetre ruler.

Using this book

- There are 24 topics and 4 tests in the book. Each test covers 6 topics.
- Each topic is about a week's work.
- Do give help and encouragement. The activities should not be a chore.
- A calculator should not be used for the work in this book.
- Do let your child mark his or her own work under your supervision and correct any careless mistakes he or she might have made.
- When all the tests have been completed let your child fill in the Certificate of Achievement on the opposite page.
- Each double page has a title, explanation of the learning point, practice section and challenge section.

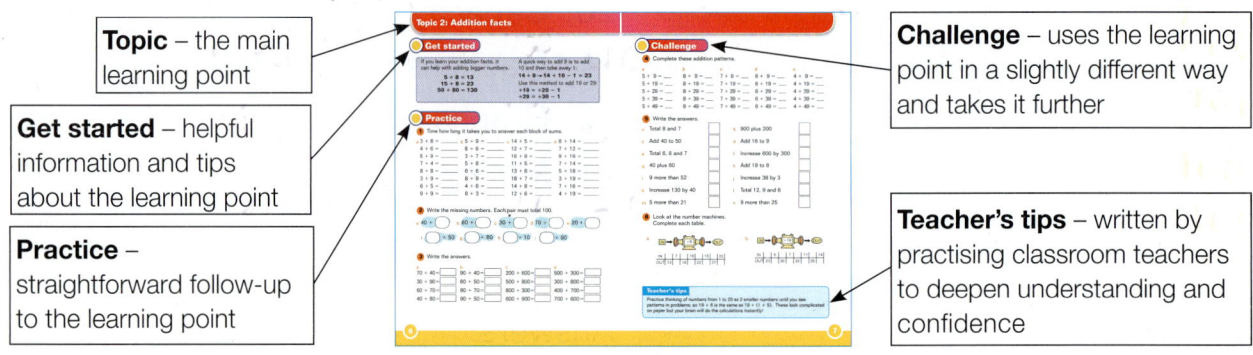

Topic – the main learning point

Get started – helpful information and tips about the learning point

Practice – straightforward follow-up to the learning point

Challenge – uses the learning point in a slightly different way and takes it further

Teacher's tips – written by practising classroom teachers to deepen understanding and confidence

This certifies that

_____

has completed

CHALLENGE MATHS YEAR 4

on _____

Scoring _____ on TEST 1

_____ on TEST 2

_____ on TEST 3

and _____ on TEST 4

Total score
out of 100 _____   40–49   good effort
50–59   well done
60–69   fantastic
70–100 brilliant

Topic 1: Place value

Get started

There are ten digits:
0, 1, 2, 3, 4, 5, 6, 7, 8 and **9**.
The position of a digit in a number gives its value.

The number **7283** is a four-digit number:
7000 + 200 + 80 + 3
↑   ↑   ↑   ↑
thousands hundreds tens units

Practice

1 Write these in figures.

a two thousand, one hundred _2100_

b nine thousand, one hundred and eighty-four _9184_

c one thousand, four hundred and eighty _1480_

d six thousand, two hundred and six _6206_

e five thousand, six hundred and eighty _5680_

f four thousand, nine hundred and thirty-five _4935_

g eight thousand and fifty-seven _8057_

h six thousand and ninety-two _6092_

i three thousand and one _3001_

j one thousand and nine _1009_

2 Write the missing numbers.

a 4687 = 4000 + _600_ + 80 + 7

b 8145 = 8000 + _100_ + _40_ + _5_

c 3298 = _3000_ + _200_ + _90_ + _8_

d 6135 = _6000_ + 100 + 30 + 5

e 9387 = _9000_ + _300_ + 80 + _7_

f 9834 = _9000_ + _800_ + _30_ + _4_

g 1499 = 1000 + _400_ + _90_ + 9

h 2598 = 2000 + _500_ + _90_ + _8_

i 4689 = _4000_ + 600 + 80 + _9_

j 7894 = _7000_ + 800 + _90_ + _4_

k 5894 = _5000_ + _800_ + 90 + 4

l 2946 = _2000_ + _900_ + _4_ + _6_

Teacher's tips

A quick way to see the value of a digit in a number is to change all the other digits to zero. To find the value of '8' in 98642 change to 08000 – '8' represents '8 thousand' in this instance.

Challenge

3 Write these numbers in order, starting with the smallest.

a 3248 4966 4769 3099 4796   3099 3248 4769 4769 4796
b 3445 3546 3080 3550 4992   3080 3445 3546 3550 4992
c 6097 6977 6009 7102 6109   6009 6097 6109 6977 7102
d 4559 4200 4560 4020 4399   4020 4200 4399 4559 4560
e 8329 8932 8900 8392 8090   8090 8329 8392 8900 8932
f 5002 5202 5222 5020 5022   5002 5020 5022 5202 5222

4 Write the value of each bold digit.

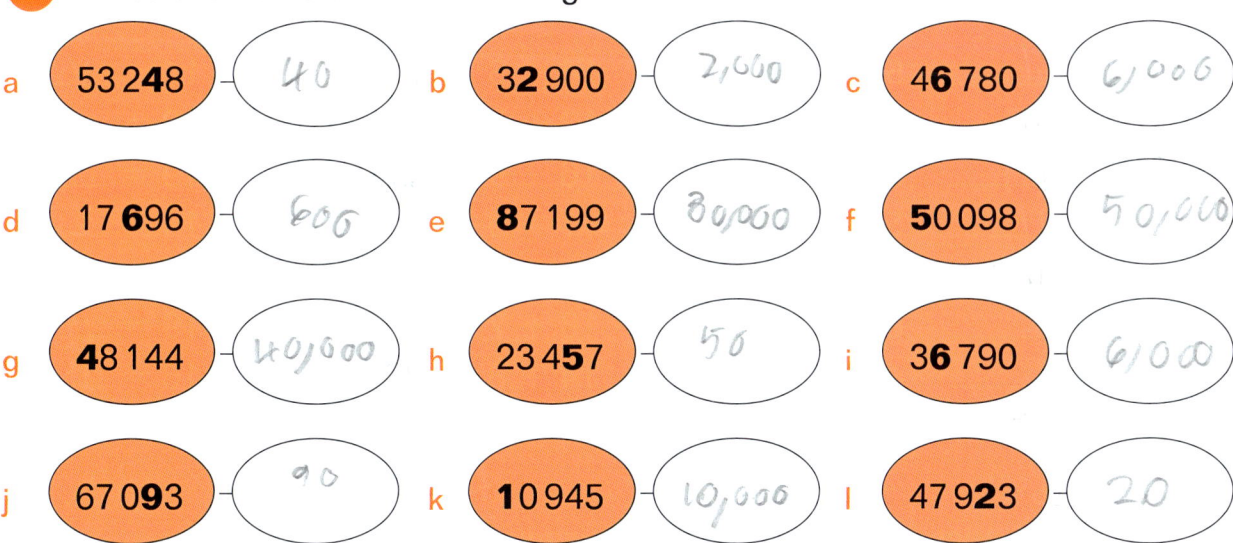

a 53 2**4**8 — 40   b 3**2** 900 — 2,000   c 4**6** 780 — 6,000

d 17 **6**96 — 600   e **8**7 199 — 80,000   f **5**0 098 — 50,000

g **4**8 144 — 40,000   h 23 4**5**7 — 50   i 3**6** 790 — 6,000

j 67 0**9**3 — 90   k **1**0 945 — 10,000   l 47 9**2**3 — 20

5 Arrange these four digits to make ten different numbers.

9, 3, 8, 4

9384   9483   4339   8439   3489
8493   4893   3948   3984   3849

Write the numbers in order, starting with the smallest.

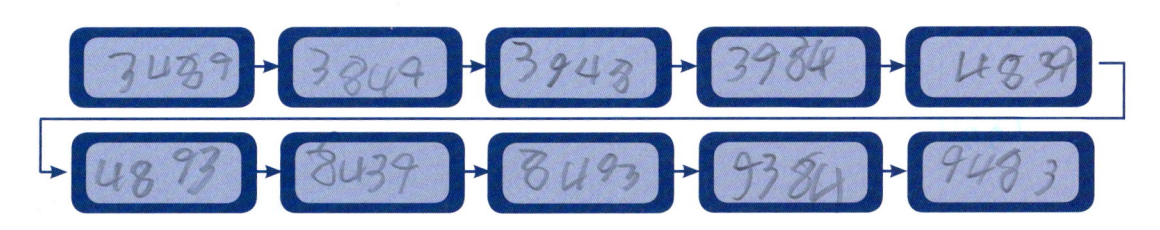

3489 → 3849 → 3948 → 3984 → 4839 →
4893 → 8439 → 8493 → 9384 → 9483

Topic 2: Addition facts

Get started

If you learn your addition facts, it can help with adding bigger numbers.

5 + 8 = 13
15 + 8 = 23
50 + 80 = 130

A quick way to add 9 is to add 10 and then take away 1:

14 + 9 → 14 + 10 − 1 = 23

Use this method to add 19 or 29:
+19 = +20 − 1
+29 = +30 − 1

Practice

1 Time how long it takes you to answer each block of sums.

a 3 + 8 = 11
   4 + 6 = 10
   5 + 9 = 14
   7 + 4 = 11
   8 + 8 = 16
   3 + 9 = 12
   6 + 5 = 11
   9 + 9 = 18
   23 sec

b 5 + 9 = 14
   8 + 6 = 14
   3 + 7 = 10
   5 + 8 = 13
   6 + 6 = 12
   8 + 9 = 17
   4 + 6 = 10
   8 + 3 = 11
   43 sec

c 14 + 5 = 19
   12 + 7 = 19
   16 + 9 = 25
   11 + 5 = 16
   13 + 8 = 21
   18 + 7 = 25
   14 + 8 = 22
   12 + 6 = 18
   12.34

d 6 + 14 = 20
   7 + 12 = 19
   9 + 19 = 28
   7 + 14 = 21
   5 + 18 = 23
   3 + 19 = 22
   7 + 16 = 23
   4 + 19 = 23
   32

2 Write the missing numbers. Each pair must total 100.

a 40 + 60   b 60 + 40   c 30 + 70   d 70 + 30   e 20 + 80

f 50 + 50   g 20 + 80   h 90 + 10   i 10 + 90

3 Write the answers.

a
70 + 40 = 110
30 + 90 = 120
60 + 70 = 130
40 + 80 = 120

b
90 + 40 = 130
60 + 50 = 110
80 + 70 = 150
90 + 50 = 140

c
200 + 600 = 800
500 + 800 = 1300
800 + 300 = 1100
600 + 900 = 1500

d
500 + 300 = 800
300 + 800 = 1100
400 + 700 = 1100
700 + 600 = 1300

 **Challenge**

4 Complete these addition patterns.

a	b	c	d	e
5 + 9 = 14	8 + 9 = 17	7 + 9 = 16	6 + 9 = 15	4 + 9 = 13
5 + 19 = 24	8 + 19 = 27	7 + 19 = 26	6 + 19 = 25	4 + 19 = 23
5 + 29 = 94	8 + 29 = 37	7 + 29 = 36	6 + 29 = 35	4 + 29 = 33
5 + 39 = 44	8 + 39 = 47	7 + 39 = 46	6 + 39 = 45	4 + 39 = 43
5 + 49 = 54	8 + 49 = 57	7 + 49 = 56	6 + 49 = 50	4 + 49 = 53

5 Write the answers.

a	Total 8 and 7	15	b	900 plus 200	1160
c	Add 40 to 50	90	d	Add 16 to 9	25
e	Total 6, 8 and 7	21	f	Increase 600 by 300	900
g	40 plus 60	100	h	Add 19 to 8	27
i	9 more than 52	61	j	Increase 38 by 3	41
k	Increase 130 by 40	170	l	Total 12, 9 and 6	27
m	5 more than 21	26	n	9 more than 25	34

6 Look at the number machines. Complete each table.

a

IN	4	7	9	16	7	15	18	23
OUT	13	16	18	25	22	24	27	32

b

IN	4	8	1	7	21	11	5	14
OUT	23	27	20	28	32	30	26	33

Teacher's tips

Practise thinking of numbers from 1 to 20 as 2 smaller numbers until you see patterns in problems; so 19 + 6 is the same as 19 + (1 + 5). These look complicated on paper but your brain will do the calculations instantly!

7

Topic 3: Subtraction facts

Get started

If you learn your subtraction facts, it can help with taking away bigger numbers.

8 − 3 = 5
18 − 3 = 15
80 − 30 = 50

A quick way to take away 9 is to take away 10 and then add 1:

26 − 9 → 26 − 10 + 1 = 17

Use this method to subtract 19 or 29:
−19 = −20 + 1
−29 = −30 + 1

Practice

1 Time how long it takes you to answer each block of sums.

a 17 − 6 = 11
   15 − 8 = 7
   16 − 9 = 7
   13 − 5 = 8
   18 − 7 = 11
   19 − 4 = 15
   14 − 6 = 8
   15 − 9 = 6
   18 − 5 = 13
   17 − 9 = 8

b 19 − 9 = 10
   13 − 7 = 6
   17 − 8 = 9
   14 − 5 = 9
   18 − 9 = 9
   16 − 7 = 9
   13 − 8 = 5
   19 − 5 = 14
   16 − 8 = 8
   15 − 7 = 8

c 24 − 8 = 16
   27 − 4 = 23
   26 − 9 = 17
   22 − 5 = 17
   23 − 6 = 17
   28 − 7 = 21
   24 − 6 = 18
   29 − 8 = 21
   21 − 5 = 16
   27 − 9 = 18

d 32 − 4 = 28
   35 − 7 = 28
   37 − 9 = 28
   33 − 8 = 25
   38 − 6 = 32
   36 − 8 = 28
   33 − 9 = 24
   34 − 5 = 29
   36 − 7 = 29
   35 − 6 = 29

2 Write the difference between each pair of numbers.

a 90, 40 → 50
   30, 60 → 30
   40, 70 → 30
   90, 80 → 10
   60, 20 → 40

b 190, 60 → 130
   80, 150 → 70
   90, 130 → 40
   140, 60 → 80
   50, 170 → 120

c 300, 600 → 300
   500, 900 → 400
   700, 200 → 500
   500, 800 → 300
   600, 900 → 300

d 1800, 300 → 1500
   500, 1600 → 1100
   600, 1700 → 1100
   1200, 900 → 300
   1500, 800 → 700

Challenge

3 Complete each of these.

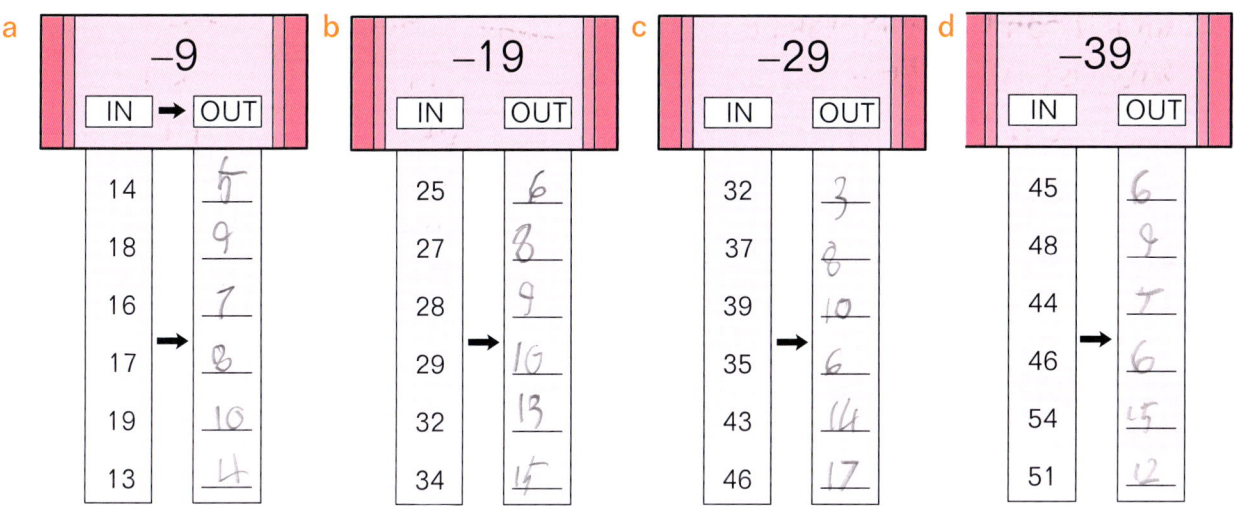

4 Write the answers.

a 15 subtract 7   8
b 80 take away 30   50
c 13 minus 8   5
d 50 minus 20   30
e 14 take away 6   8
f Reduce 90 by 20   70
g Decrease 12 by 4   8
h 70 subtract 30   40
i Reduce 16 by 9   7
j The difference between 600 and 200   400
k The difference between 8 and 19   11
l Decrease 900 by 400   500

5 Complete each number trail from 100 to zero.

a 100 −30→ 70 −50→ 20 −14→ 6 −6→ 0

b 100 −20→ 80 −70→ 10 −6→ 4 −4→ 0

c 100 −25→ 75 −15→ 60 −45→ 15 −15→ 0

d 100 −5→ 95 −55→ 40 −35→ 5 −5→ 0

Teacher's tips

To find the difference between two numbers quickly, subtract the smaller number from the larger one.

Topic 4: Length

Get started

Length is measured in **millimetres**, **centimetres**, **metres** and **kilometres**.

1 kilometre (km) = 1000 metres (m)
1 metre (m) = 100 centimetres (cm)
1 centimetre (cm) = 10 millimetres (mm)

855 cm = 8.55 m

The point separates the metres from the centimetres.

Practice

1 Write these lengths.

a 5000 m = _5_ km
b 10000 m = _10_ km
c 3500 m = _35_ km
d 500 m = _½_ km
e 6 km = _6000_ m
f 2000 cm = _20_ m
g 7.5 km = _7005_ m
h 525 cm = _5¼_ m
i 200 cm = _2_ m
j 7 cm = _70_ mm
k 650 cm = _650_ m
l 6.35 m = _60.35_ cm
m 40 mm = _4_ cm
n 1.2 km = _1260_ m
o 15 mm = _1.5_ cm

2 Use a ruler to measure.

a Measure these lines in centimetres.

_6_ cm

_4_ cm

_5_ cm

_3_ cm

b Measure these in centimetres and then write each length in millimetres.

4½ cm = _45_ mm

2½ cm = _25_ mm

6½ cm = _65_ mm

5½ cm = _55_ mm

Teacher's tips

Convert all the measurements into the same unit before solving the problem – normally the smallest is simplest as they will all be whole numbers. Then convert back into the most appropriate unit to express the answer.

Challenge

3 Measure these pencils and write their lengths in millimetres.

a 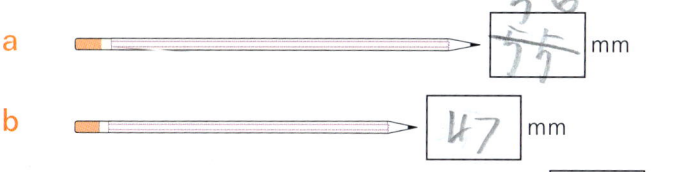 56 / 57 mm

b 47 mm

c 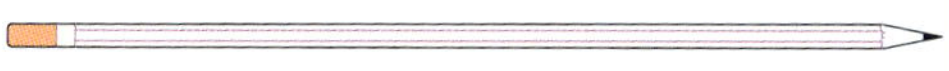 64 mm

d  36 mm

4 Write the answers.

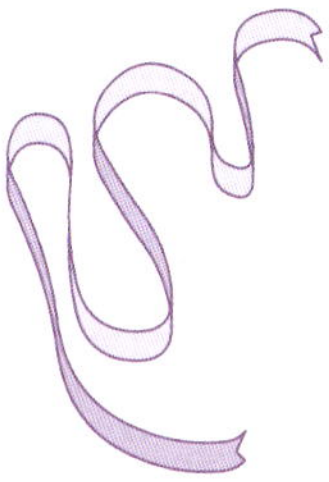

a A piece of ribbon is 45 cm long. 100 mm is cut off. How long is the piece of ribbon now? 35 cm

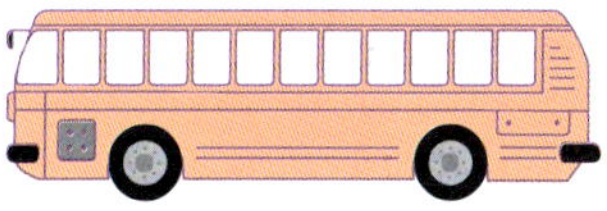

b A bus travels 4.5 km from Arnely to Boseworth. How far does it travel in total on a return journey? 9 KM

c What is 500 m less than 6 km? 5.500 KM

d Two shelves are 70 cm and 90 cm in length. What is their total length in metres and centimetres? 1.6 M 160 cm

e A tree is 3.5 m tall. It doubles in height in a year. What is its height in centimetres after a year? 700 cm / 7M

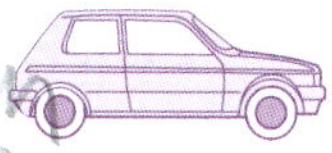

f A family sets off to drive 480 km. After 250 km how much further have they to go? 230KM 230KM 23 KM

5 Look at this ruler. What is the distance between the arrows?

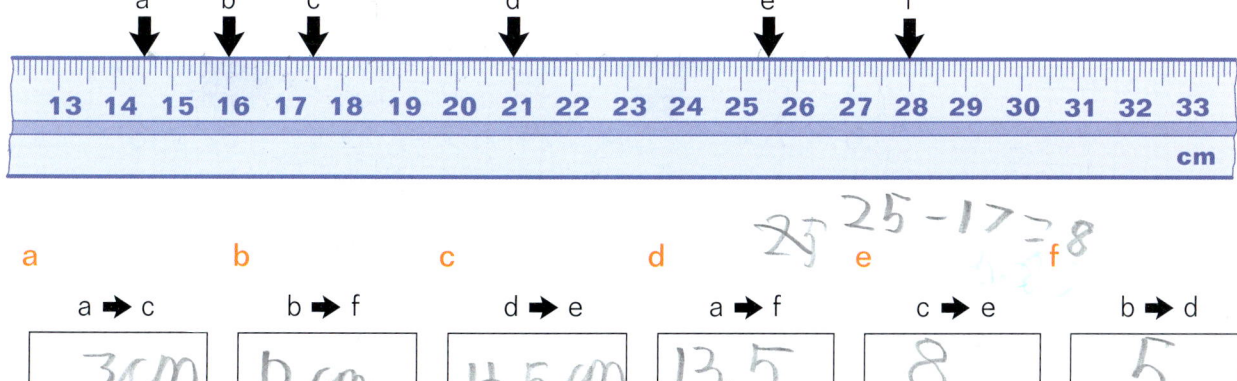

a	b	c	d	e	f
a→c	b→f	d→e	a→f	c→e	b→d
3 cm	12 cm	4.5 cm	13.5	8	5

25 25-17=8

11

Topic 5: Multiplication and division facts

Get started

If you know your multiplication facts, it helps you learn the division facts.

For every fact, you can work out another three facts very easily. Look at this for the trio 4, 6 and 24:

4 × 6 = 24
6 × 4 = 24 ← Remember **6 × 4** and **4 × 6** give the same answer – it doesn't matter which way round you multiply.
24 ÷ 4 = 6
24 ÷ 6 = 4

Practice

1 Write the missing numbers for each trio.

a ⟨7, 5, 35⟩ ⟨5 × 7 = 35⟩ ⟨7 × 5 = 35⟩ ⟨35 ÷ 5 = 7⟩ ⟨35 ÷ 7 = 5⟩
b ⟨4, 9, 36⟩ ⟨9 × 4 = 36⟩ ⟨4 × 9 = 36⟩ ⟨36 ÷ 9 = 4⟩ ⟨36 ÷ 4 = 9⟩
c ⟨3, 6, 18⟩ ⟨6 × 3 = 18⟩ ⟨3 × 6 = 18⟩ ⟨18 ÷ 6 = 3⟩ ⟨18 ÷ 3 = 6⟩
d ⟨6, 5, 30⟩ ⟨5 × 6 = 30⟩ ⟨6 × 5 = 30⟩ ⟨30 ÷ 5 = 6⟩ ⟨30 ÷ 6 = 5⟩
e ⟨9, 3, 27⟩ ⟨9 × 3 = 27⟩ ⟨3 × 9 = 27⟩ ⟨27 ÷ 3 = 9⟩ ⟨27 ÷ 9 = 3⟩
f ⟨7, 6, 42⟩ ⟨7 × 6 = 42⟩ ⟨6 × 7 = 42⟩ ⟨42 ÷ 7 = 6⟩ ⟨42 ÷ 6 = 7⟩
g ⟨8, 9, 72⟩ ⟨8 × 9 = 72⟩ ⟨9 × 8 = 72⟩ ⟨72 ÷ 8 = 9⟩ ⟨72 ÷ 9 = 8⟩

2 Time how long it takes you to answer each block.
Try to beat your best time.

a 9 × 5 = 45   b 3 × 6 = 18   c 35 ÷ 5 = 7   d 36 ÷ 6 = 6
   6 × 4 = 24   6 × 7 = 42   21 ÷ 7 = 3   32 ÷ 8 = 4
   8 × 8 = 64   5 × 4 = 20   45 ÷ 9 = 5   28 ÷ 4 = 7
   3 × 9 = 27   4 × 8 = 32   30 ÷ 6 = 10   36 ÷ 9 = 4
   3 × 8 = 24   7 × 7 = 49   24 ÷ 8 = 3   21 ÷ 3 = 7
   4 × 6 = 24   3 × 7 = 21   18 ÷ 3 = 6   14 ÷ 7 = 2
   6 × 5 = 30   5 × 8 = 40   45 ÷ 5 = 9   20 ÷ 5 = 4

12

Challenge

3 Complete each table for these machines.

a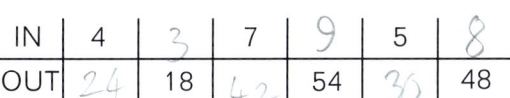

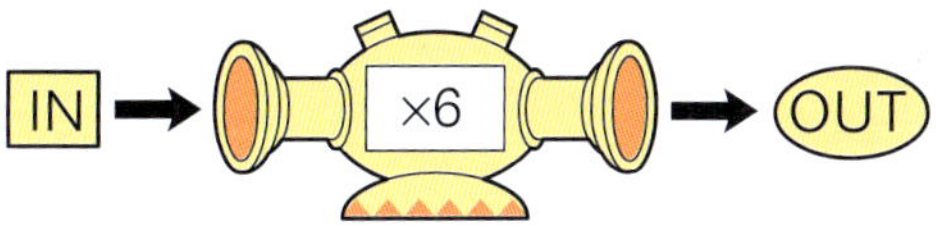

IN	4	3	7	9	5	8
OUT	24	18	42	54	30	48

b

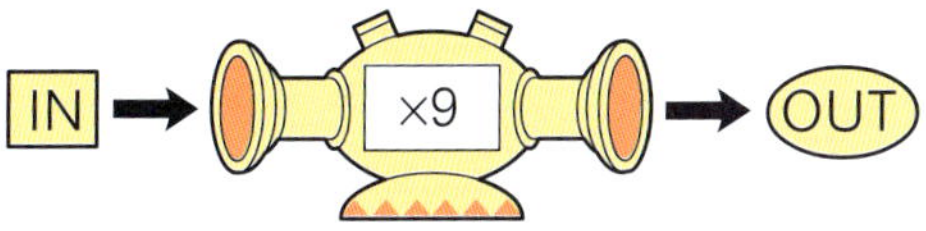

IN		6		7		4
OUT	45			18		81

c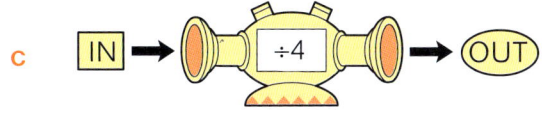

IN	28		36		16	
OUT		3		8		5

d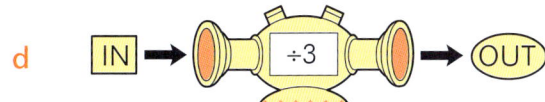

IN		21		15		24
OUT	6		9		4	

4 Complete these grids.

a

×	6	8	4
3	18	27	2
9	54	72	36
2	12	16	8

b

×	4	9	3
8			
7			
5	20		

c

×	4	6	7
2	8		
5	20		
8			

d

×	4		8
	8	10	
3	12		24
6		30	

e

×	3	7	
4	12	28	36
		21		63
	24	56	

f

×		6	
	12	18	30
5	20	30	50
	40	60	100

Teacher's tips

Construct a multiplication/division triangle by writing the two numbers being multiplied in the bottom two corners, and the answer in the top of the triangle. When dividing the top number by either of the bottom numbers, the unused number is the answer.

Topic 6: 2D shapes

Get started

A **polygon** is any 2D shape with straight sides. The sides and angles of a **regular polygon** are all equal. These are the names of some polygons.

Triangle	3 sides		**Heptagon**	7 sides	
Quadrilateral	4 sides		**Octagon**	8 sides	
Pentagon	5 sides		**Nonagon**	9 sides	
Hexagon	6 sides		**Decagon**	10 sides	

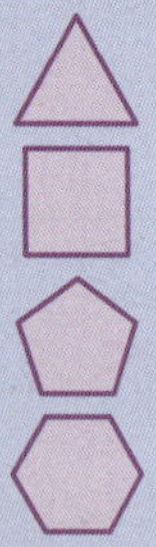

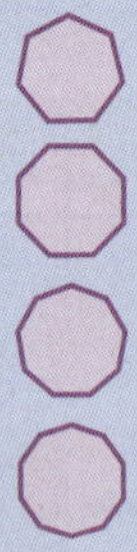

Some shapes have more than one name.

For example a **rectangle** is a quadrilateral with four right angles.

A **square** is a special rectangle because the four sides are equal.

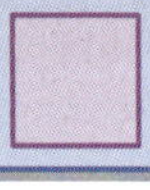

Practice

1 Write one name for each shape. Tick the regular polygons.

a. Triangle
b. Triangle
c. Quadrilateral
d. Hexagon
e. hexagon

f. Triangle
g. Quadrilateral
h. Quadrilateral
i. Pentagon
j. Quadrilateral

k. Quadrilateral
l. Octagon
m. Decagon
n. Nonagon
o. Octagon

14

Challenge

2 Tick the odd one out in each set. Complete each sentence.

a All _Pentagons_ have 5 sides.
b All _Quadrilateral_ have 4 sides.
c All _Heptagons_ have 7 sides.
d All _Triangles_ have 3 sides.
e All _Nonagons_ have 9 sides.
f All _Octagons_ have 8 sides.

3 Join each shape to its correct place on the Carroll diagram.

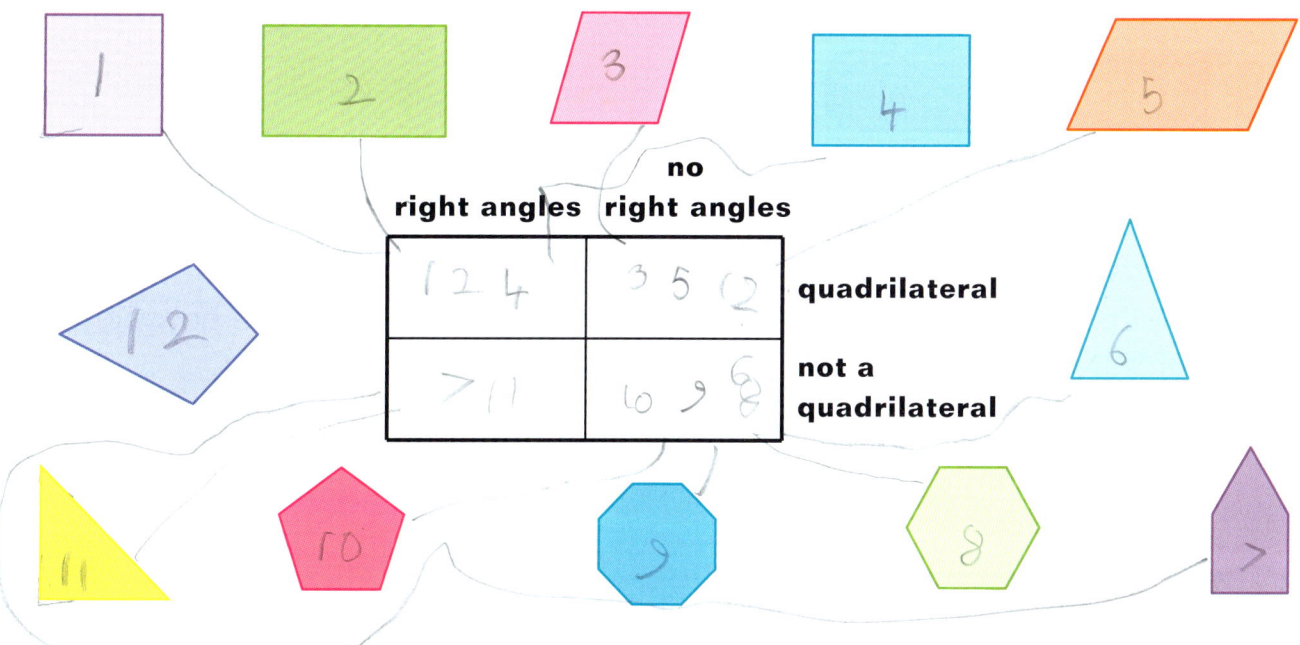

	right angles	no right angles
quadrilateral	1 2 4	3 5
not a quadrilateral	7 11	6 9 8

Teacher's tips

A good way to remember that a right angle is 90° is to hold your right hand up with the fingers together and thumb stretched out – the angle the fingers and thumb make is a right angle.

15

Test 1: (Score 1 mark for every correct answer)

Topic 1

handwritten at top: 6000 6,100 6,100 6010

1 Write this in figures:

six thousand and forty-seven [6047]

2 Write the missing numbers.

7264 = __2000__ + __200__ + 60 + 4

3 Write these in order starting with the smallest.

6704 7064 6740 7604 6047

handwritten: 6047 6704 6740 7064 7604

4 Write the value of the bold digit:

6**2**078 __60__

Topic 2

5 Complete this addition pattern:

5 + 9 = [14]
15 + 9 = [24]
25 + 9 = [34]

6 Write the missing number.

[8] + 7 = 15

7 Write the total. 40 + 80 = [20]

8 What is the total of 5, 8 and 7? [20]

Topic 3

9 Write the missing number.

[13] − 7 = 6

10 What is 120 subtract 50?

[20]

11 Write the number coming out of this machine.

IN 35 → −19 → [16]

12 Write the difference between this pair of numbers.

1500, 600 → [900]

Topic 4

13 Write the missing lengths.
80 mm = __8__ cm
6500 m = __6 and ½__ km

14 Write this length in cm and mm.

_____ [ ] cm = [ ] mm

16

15 Write the length of this pencil. _____

16 What is the difference in length between two lines measuring 17 cm and 9 cm? ☐

Topic 5

17 Write the missing numbers for this trio:

⟨8, 4, 32⟩ ⟨__ × 4 = __⟩ ⟨__ × __ = 32⟩ ⟨__ ÷ 4 = __⟩ ⟨32 ÷ __ = __⟩

18 Answer these. 7 × 6 = ☐   32 ÷ 4 = ☐

19 Complete the table for this machine.

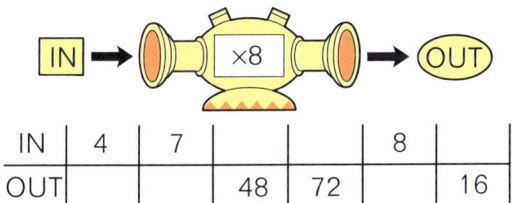

IN	4	7			8	
OUT			48	72		16

20 Complete this grid.

x	3	8
4		
		48
9		63

Topic 6

21 Name these shapes. _____

Tick the regular shape.

22 Write two names for this shape.

_____
_____

23 Tick the odd one out.

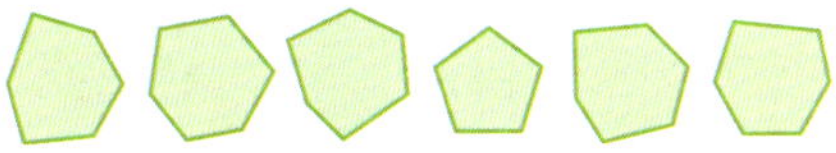

24 Tick the right angles.

Mark the test. Remember to fill in your score on page 3.

Write your score out of 24. ☐

Add a bonus point if you scored 20 or more.

TOTAL SCORE FOR TEST 1   ☐

> **Teacher's tips**
>
> In tests, take your time and make sure you read the question carefully. If you're not sure about a question leave it out and come back to it at the end. Always check your answers before finishing the test!

17

Topic 7: Time

Get started

Mornings and afternoons are shown by **a.m.** and **p.m.**

60 seconds = 1 minute

60 minutes = 1 hour

24 hours = 1 day

Twenty-past seven in the morning ➔ **7.20 a.m.**

Twenty-past seven in the evening ➔ **7.20 p.m.**

Practice

1 Write the time shown by each clock.

a    b    c    d

e    f    g    h

2 Draw hands to show these times.

a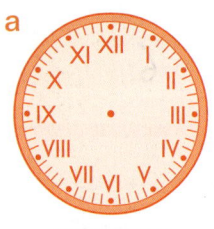

b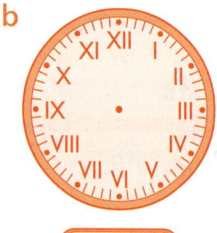

c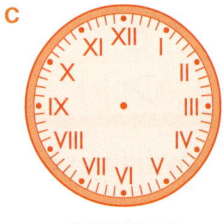

d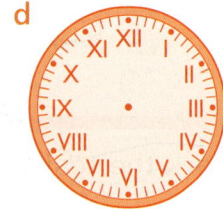

Teacher's tips

Some people find reading digital clocks backwards helps make clearer what time it is, replacing the ':' or '.' with 'past'. So read 11.42 as '42 minutes past 11'.

Challenge

3 A coach takes 25 minutes between each stop. Complete the timetable.

Church Street	8.50 a.m.	9.35 a.m.	11.00 a.m.	1.05 p.m.
Marsh Lane	9.15 a.m.			
Hospital			11.50 a.m.	
Swimming pool				2.20 p.m.

4 Answer these time problems.

a   A film started at the cinema at 6.35 p.m. If it lasted for 90 minutes, what time did it finish? _____

b   Tom wakes up at 7.30 a.m. If school begins at 8.55 a.m., how long has he got before it starts? _____

c   A football match lasts for 45 minutes each half, with a 15-minute break at half time. If the match starts at 11.30 a.m., what time will it finish? _____

d   A swimming session lasted 1 hour and 20 minutes. If it finished at 2.45 p.m., when did the session start? _____

e   A car journey started at 9.45 a.m. and finished at 3.50 p.m. How long did the journey last? _____

5 These clocks are all running slow. If the real time is 4.45, how many minutes slow is each clock?

a
_____ minutes slow

b
_____ minutes slow

c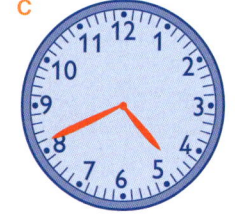
_____ minutes slow

d
_____ minutes slow

e
_____ minutes slow

f
_____ minutes slow

Topic 8: Fractions of shapes

Get started

A fraction has two parts:
$\frac{2}{3}$ ← **numerator** (top number)
   ← **denominator** (bottom number)

1 part out of 3 shaded.
This shows $\frac{1}{3}$.

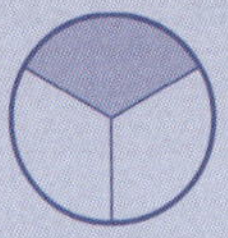

2 parts out of 3 shaded.
This shows $\frac{2}{3}$.

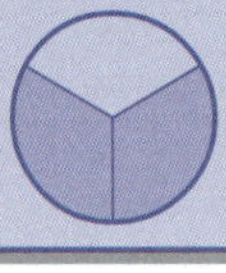

Fractions that have the same value are called **equivalent fractions**.

$\frac{1}{2}$ is the same as $\frac{2}{4}$

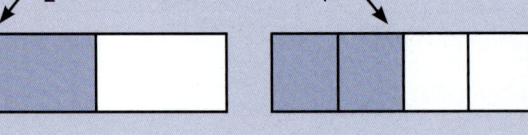

Practice

1 Write the fraction coloured on each shape.

a 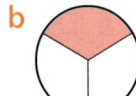   b    c    d    e 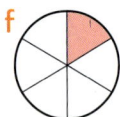   f (circle with 6 parts, 1 shaded)

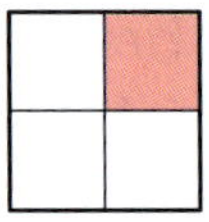

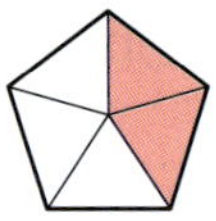

g 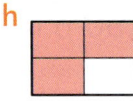   h    i 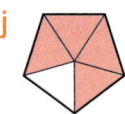   j 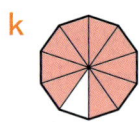   k 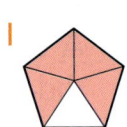   l (pentagon)

2 Write the equivalent fractions.

a 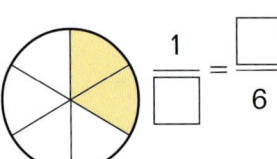 $\frac{1}{\square} = \frac{\square}{6}$

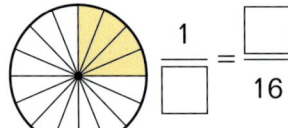 $\frac{1}{\square} = \frac{\square}{16}$

b 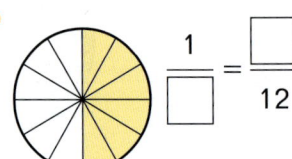 $\frac{1}{\square} = \frac{\square}{12}$

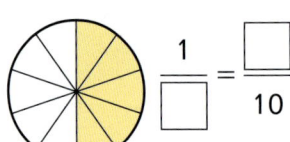 $\frac{1}{\square} = \frac{\square}{10}$

c 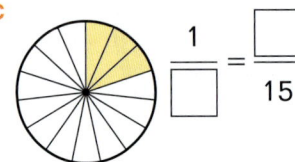 $\frac{1}{\square} = \frac{\square}{15}$

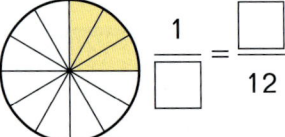 $\frac{1}{\square} = \frac{\square}{12}$

Challenge

3 Write the fraction shaded.

a  b  c 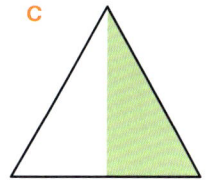 d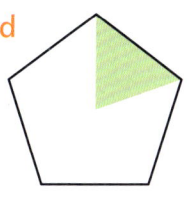

_____ _____ _____ _____

e 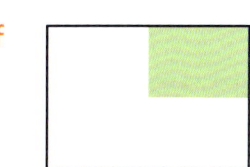 f

4 Shade these strips to show the fractions.

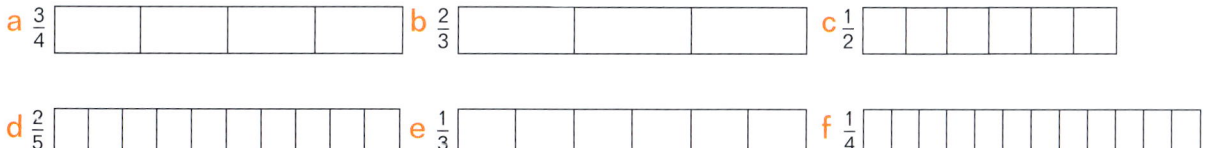

a $\frac{3}{4}$ b $\frac{2}{3}$ c $\frac{1}{2}$

d $\frac{2}{5}$ e $\frac{1}{3}$ f $\frac{1}{4}$

5 Write these fractions in order, starting with the smallest.

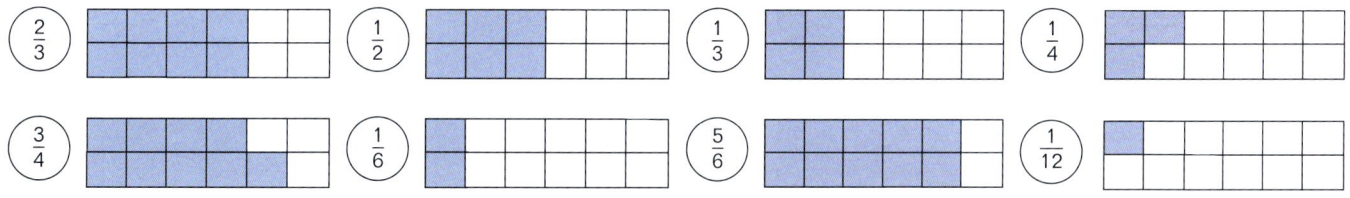

_____ _____ _____ _____ _____ _____ _____ _____

Teacher's tips

The line in a proper fraction means 'out of every'. Reading fractions aloud using this method helps when writing equivalent fractions.

Topic 9: Addition

Get started

There are lots of different ways to add up numbers in your head. One way is to break up numbers to make them easier to add.

For example: **46 + 37**

Try using these three steps:
1. Hold the bigger number in your head: 46
2. Add the tens: 46 + 30 = 76
3. Add the units: 76 + 7 = 83

Practice

1 Look at these letter codes. Work out the different totals.

a 60   b 40   c 80   d 50   e 35   f 55   g 25   h 75

a a + d → _____   b a + g → _____   c e + g → _____
d b + c → _____   e e + c → _____   f f + e → _____
g c + d → _____   h h + d → _____   i h + g → _____
j b + a → _____   k g + c → _____   l f + h → _____

2 Work these out in your head.

a 45 + 50 =   b 60 + 55 =   c 80 + 43 =   d 28 + 70 =

e 90 + 67 =   f 42 + 34 =   g 23 + 65 =   h 43 + 36 =

i 57 + 33 =   j 61 + 28 =   k 58 + 34 =   l 57 + 25 =

m 63 + 28 =   n 42 + 49 =   o 54 + 27 =   p 74 + 52 =

q 62 + 85 =   r 55 + 76 =   s 83 + 58 =   t 74 + 68 =

Teacher's tips

When trying to take a total from two numbers look at the units first. Will the sum of the units in the two numbers give the number of units you're looking for? Remember, you may have to carry the 10.

Challenge

3 Add the rows and fill in the yellow boxes. Add the columns and fill in the pink boxes. Add the numbers in the yellow boxes, then add the numbers in the pink boxes. The two totals are the same. Write this in the blue box.

a
53	47	
28	31	

b
31	67	
42	39	

c
62	57	
38	29	

d
62	53	
74	47	

4 Join each number on the left with a number on the right to make a total of 111.

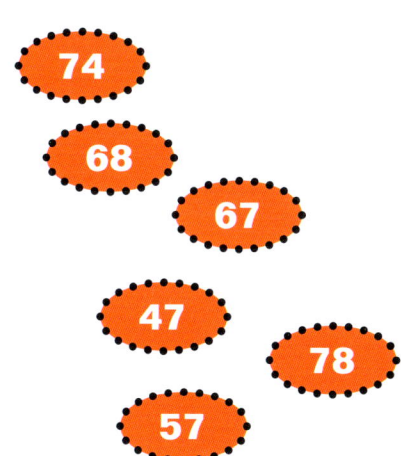
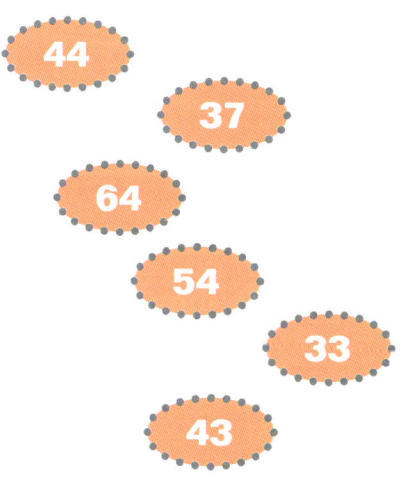

5 Write the missing digits 3 to 8 to complete these. Use each digit only once.

a 28 + ◯7 = 9◯

b 59 + ◯4 = 1◯3

c ◯1 + 6◯ = 145

Topic 10: Subtraction

Get started

There are lots of different ways to subtract numbers in your head.

One way is to find the difference by counting on from the smaller number.

This number line shows the method to work out **84 − 47**.

Count on from 47 to 50. Hold the 3 in your head.

50 to 84 is 34.

34 + 3 is 37.

So **84 − 47 = 37**

Practice

1 Draw the jumps on the number lines to help answer these.

a 74 − 36 = ☐   36 ─────────────── 74

b 83 − 46 = ☐   46 ─────────────── 83

c 61 − 37 = ☐   37 ─────────────── 61

d 73 − 49 = ☐   49 ─────────────── 73

e 45 − 28 = ☐   28 ─────────────── 45

f 85 − 57 = ☐   57 ─────────────── 85

g 72 − 46 = ☐   46 ─────────────── 72

h 67 − 38 = ☐   38 ─────────────── 67

i 81 − 64 = ☐   64 ─────────────── 81

j 92 − 57 = ☐   57 ─────────────── 92

Challenge

2 Do these in your head.

a 58 − 37 =   b 74 − 41 =   c 85 − 63 =   d 76 − 32 =
e 87 − 53 =   f 52 − 18 =   g 43 − 16 =   h 61 − 14 =
i 57 − 19 =   j 72 − 17 =   k 64 − 28 =   l 42 − 25 =
m 53 − 28 =   n 56 − 29 =   o 65 − 27 =   p 94 − 57 =
q 72 − 45 =   r 85 − 46 =   s 93 − 68 =   t 84 − 58 =

3 Write the difference between the two numbers in the middle circle.

a 36 ← ○ → 54   b 29 ← ○ → 45   c 62 ← ○ → 71   d 51 ← ○ → 67
e 28 ← ○ → 56   f 67 ← ○ → 84   g 45 ← ○ → 61   h 67 ← ○ → 92

4 Join each number on the left with a number on the right to make a difference of 44.

93, 62, 83, 52, 33, 53 | 49, 77, 97, 96, 18, 39

5 Write the missing digits 3 to 8 to complete these. Use each digit only once.

3 4 5 6 7 8

a 8○ − ○7 = 26   b 9○ − ○8 = 26   c ○4 − 4○ = 26

Teacher's tips

When subtracting mentally start with the units and work through tens, hundreds etc. Round a number to the nearest 10 if it helps, just remember to make the adjustment to the answer so your rounding is cancelled out.

25

Topic 11: Sequences and patterns

Get started

A number **sequence** is a list of numbers in a pattern. To find the rule or pattern in a sequence it can help to find the differences between each pair of numbers.

$1 \xrightarrow{+4} 5 \xrightarrow{+4} 9 \xrightarrow{+4} 13$

The rule or pattern is **+4**

$32 \xrightarrow{-3} 29 \xrightarrow{-3} 26 \xrightarrow{-3} 23$

The rule or pattern is **−3**

Practice

1 Write the next three numbers in each sequence.

a	b	c	d	e	f	g	h	i	j
7	7	117	230	85	900	14	2	55	200
9	12	119	240	80	800	17	6	52	190
11	17	121	250	75	700	20	10	49	180
13	22	123	260	70	600	23	14	46	170

2 Write the missing three numbers in each sequence.

a	b	c	d	e	f	g	h	i	j
18			26	97	105		93		910
21	78		30		110	73		50	810
	73	510	34		115	64	85	53	
27	68	560		103		55	81	56	610
	63	610	42	105			77	59	
33		660		107	130	37			410

26

Challenge

3 Write the four missing numbers in each sequence.

a ☐, ☐, −3, −2, −1, 0, ☐, ☐

b ☐, ☐, −15, −10, −5, 0, ☐, ☐

c ☐, ☐, −4, −3, −2, −1, ☐, ☐

d ☐, ☐, −12, −9, −6, −3, ☐, ☐

e ☐, ☐, −10, −8, −6, −4, ☐, ☐

f ☐, ☐, −4, −1, 2, 5, ☐, ☐

g ☐, ☐, −7, −5, −3, −1, ☐, ☐

h ☐, ☐, −10, −6, −2, 2, ☐, ☐

4 Two numbers in each sequence have been swapped over. Circle the two numbers.

a 28, 29, 35, 31, 32, 33, 34, 30

b 15, 19, 23, 31, 27, 35, 39

c 53, 51, 43, 47, 45, 49, 41

d 480, 478, 468, 474, 472, 470, 476

e 950, 910, 930, 920, 940, 900, 890

f 150, 149, 144, 147, 146, 145, 148

5 Follow the instructions for this number square. Look for any patterns.

- Colour the square that has number 3.
- Count on three and colour the square that has number 6.
- Keep counting on three and continue the pattern.
- Circle the number 2.
- Count on two and circle 4.
- Keep counting on two and continue the pattern.

1	2	3	4	5	6	7	8
9	10	11	12	13	14	15	16
17	18	19	20	21	22	23	24
25	26	27	28	29	30	31	32
33	34	35	36	37	38	39	40
41	42	43	44	45	46	47	48
49	50	51	52	53	54	55	56
57	58	59	60	61	62	63	64

Teacher's tips

Try making up your own sequence and pattern problems for friends or family. They don't always have to be numbers. What's missing in this one for instance: M T W T F S ?

Topic 12: Comparing and ordering numbers

Get started

| When you need to put numbers in order it helps to write them under each other, lining up the units. For example:

        2370
           387
 1307
       438    387
       438
     1307
     2370 | We use < and > to compare numbers.

< means **is less than**
For example: **475 < 580**
475 is less than 580

> means **is greater than**
For example: **764 > 746**
764 is greater than 746 |

Practice

1 Write these numbers in order, starting with the smallest.

a 368, 860, 306, 380, 800, 806 _____
b 405, 590, 450, 594, 486, 589 _____
c 689, 966, 659, 965, 690, 906 _____
d 215, 512, 522, 205, 505, 520 _____
e 3125, 3502, 2599, 3005, 3152 _____
f 1706, 1670, 7611, 7509, 5799 _____
g 8345, 8543, 8095, 8307, 8079 _____
h 7324, 7244, 7323, 7332, 7342 _____

2 Write the sign < or > for each pair of numbers.

a 345 ☐ 428   b 614 ☐ 641   c 508 ☐ 505
d 617 ☐ 609   e 934 ☐ 919   f 2453 ☐ 2540
g 1800 ☐ 1798   h 4976 ☐ 4967   i 7806 ☐ 7860

Teacher's tips

Practise your number skills by dealing numbered playing cards and then arranging them into the biggest and smallest number possible. What's the biggest or smallest difference you can make by changing only 2 cards?

Challenge

3 Write the half-way number on each of these number lines.

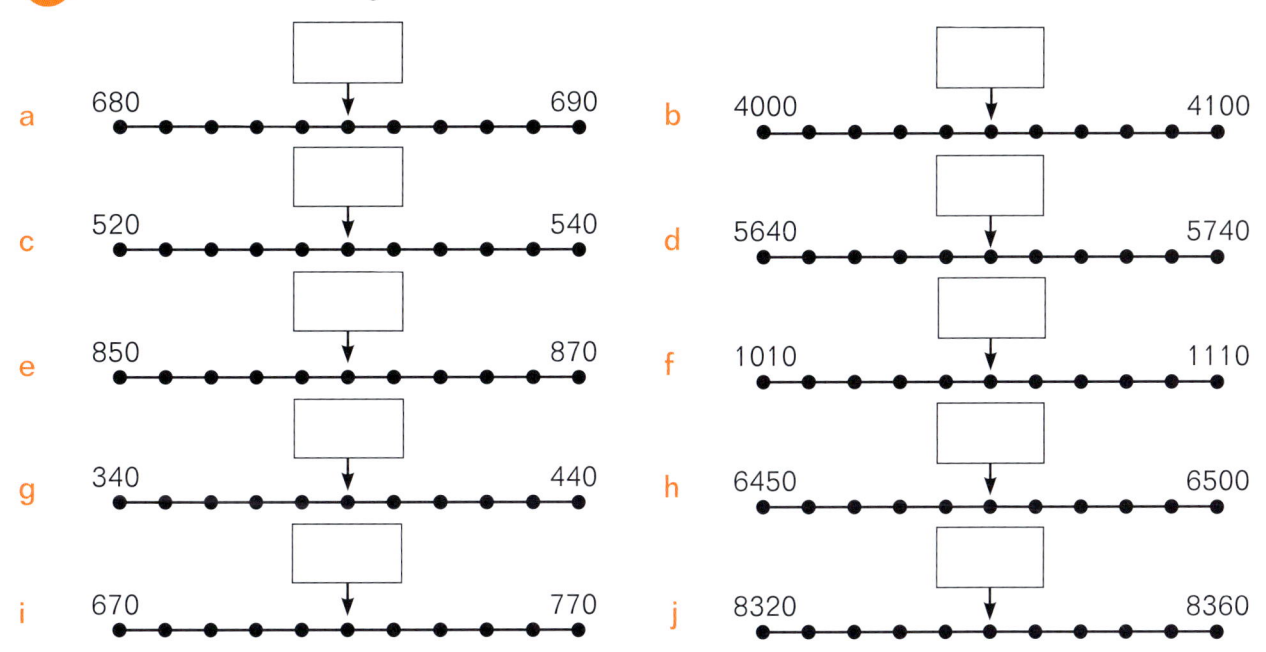

a 680 —— 690
b 4000 —— 4100
c 520 —— 540
d 5640 —— 5740
e 850 —— 870
f 1010 —— 1110
g 340 —— 440
h 6450 —— 6500
i 670 —— 770
j 8320 —— 8360

4 Write the signs < or > for these.

a 502 __ 567 __ 387
b 7400 __ 7066 __ 7060
c 2398 __ 2400 __ 2402
d 399 __ 309 __ 394
e 3654 __ 3746 __ 3577
f 6983 __ 6098 __ 5277

5 This table shows the area of some of the largest islands in Europe. Write them in size order, starting with the largest.

Island	Area (sq km)
Corsica	8 270
Crete	8 260
Cyprus	9 251
Great Britain	218 041
Iceland	103 000
Ireland	83 766
Sardinia	23 800
Sicily	25 400

Island

29

Test 2: (Score 1 mark for every correct answer)

Topic 7

1 Write the time shown.

2 Draw hands to show this time.

3 A pizza is ordered at 7.25 p.m. If it finally arrived at 8.15 p.m., how long did it take for the pizza to be delivered?

4 A clock is 25 minutes slow. If it shows 8.35, what is the real time?

Topic 8

5 Write the fraction that is shaded.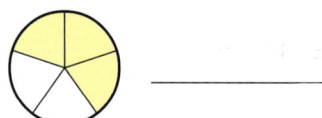

6 Write the equivalent fractions.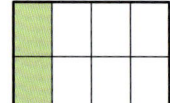

$$\frac{1}{\Box} = \frac{\Box}{8}$$

7 Write the fraction that is shaded.

8 Shade this strip to show the fraction $\frac{2}{3}$.

Topic 9

9 Write the total of these two numbers.

75 + 90 =

10 Do this in your head.

65 + 87 =

11 Add the rows, then add the columns to make the same corner total.

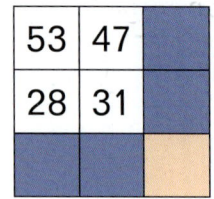

12 Circle the two numbers that total 125.

67   59

          58

    76   79

30

Topic 10

13 Answer this.

85 − 47 = ☐

14 What is the difference between 73 and 45? ☐

15 Circle the two numbers that have a difference of 48.

83 87 45 38 93

16 Write the missing digits.

7☐ − ☐6 = 26

Topic 11

17 Write the next two numbers in this sequence.

8, 13, 18, 23, ☐, ☐

18 Write the missing numbers in this sequence.

70, 61, ☐, 43, ☐, 25

19 Write the four missing numbers.

☐, ☐, −8, −5, −2, 1, ☐, ☐

20 Two numbers have been swapped. Circle the two numbers.

47, 45, 43, 37, 39, 41, 35

Topic 12

21 Write these numbers in order, starting with the smallest.

4769, 4799, 4679, 4767

_____ _____ _____ _____

22 Write the sign < or > for each pair of numbers.

6105 __ 6150   4355 __ 4335

23 Write the half-way number.

4120　　☐　　4320

24 Write the sign < or > for these.

6104 __ 3259 __ 3260

Mark the test. Remember to fill in your score on page 3.

Write your score out of 24. ☐

Add a bonus point if you scored 20 or more.

TOTAL SCORE FOR TEST 2 ☐

Topic 13: Rounding numbers

Get started

Rounding numbers – by changing them to the nearest ten or hundred – makes them easier to work with.

It is also useful for estimating approximate answers.

Rounding to the nearest 10

Look at the **units** digit.

If it is 5 or more, round up the tens digit.

If it is less than 5, the tens digit stays the same.

28<u>5</u> rounds up to 290

51<u>4</u> rounds down to 510

Rounding to the nearest 100

Look at the **tens** digits.

If it is 5 or more, round up the hundreds digit.

If it is less than 5, the hundreds digit stays the same.

42<u>6</u>1 rounds up to 4300

61<u>4</u>7 rounds down to 6100

Practice

1 Round these amounts to the nearest 10.

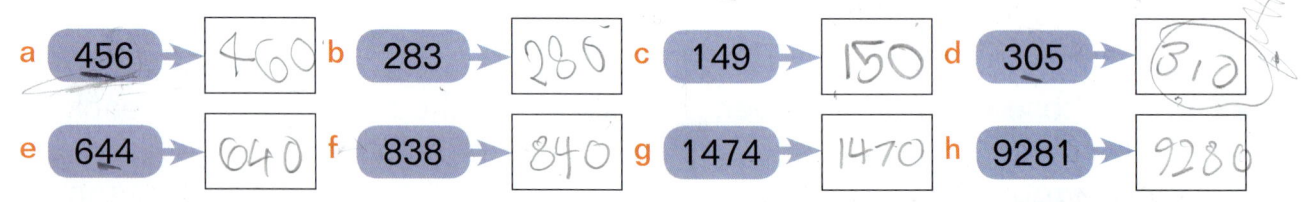

a 456 → 460   b 283 → 280   c 149 → 150   d 305 → 310

e 644 → 640   f 838 → 840   g 1474 → 1470   h 9281 → 9280

2 Round these to the nearest 100.

a 673 → 700   b 457 → 500   c 145 → 100   d 565 → 600

e 816 → 800   f 937 → 900   g 4914 → 4900   h 7845 → 7800

3 Round these amounts to the nearest pound.

a £1.46 → £1.00   b £4.53 → 5.00   c £2.09 → 2.00   d £6.27 → 6.00

e £4.63 → 5.00   f £8.50 → 9.00   g £13.08 → 13.00   h £16.49 → 16.00

Challenge

4 Estimate which tens number each arrow points to.

a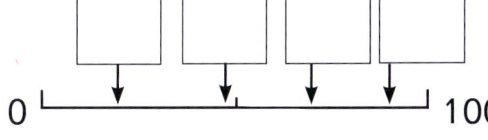

b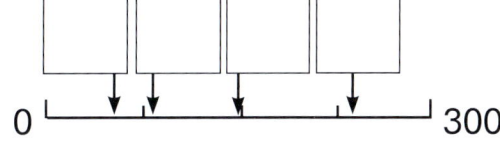

c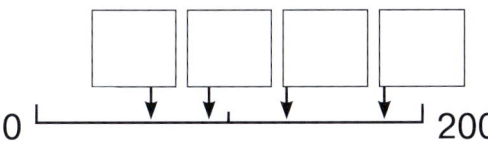

d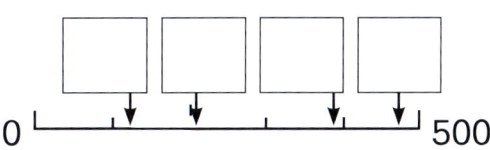

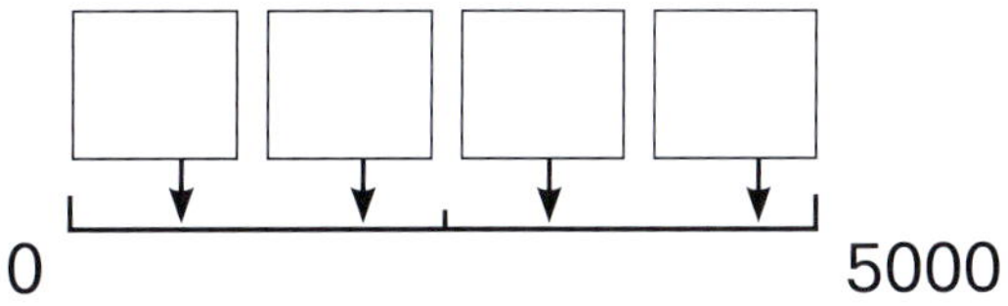

5 Estimate which hundreds number each arrow points to.

a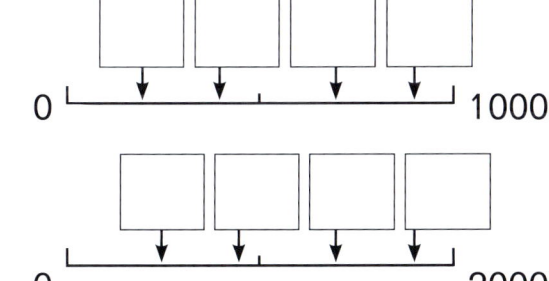

b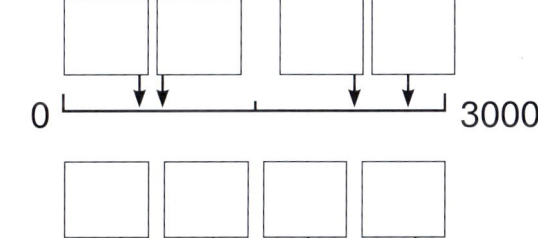

6 Estimate to give approximate answers, e.g. in a box 1 150 + 230 = 380. The first one has been done for you.

a Round these to the nearest 10.

149 + 232 → 380

308 + 434 →

593 − 418 →

746 − 338 →

33 × 19 →

47 × 22 →

b Round these to the nearest 100.

4738 + 1229 →

6163 + 3442 →

4869 − 2345 →

7351 − 4138 →

221 × 381 →

542 × 386 →

Teacher's tips

Focus on what you are rounding to – the nearest 1, 10, 100 etc. If it's to the nearest 10, you look at the units; if it's to the nearest 100 you look at the tens, and so on.

Topic 14: Weight and mass

Get started

Weight and mass are closely linked but are not quite the same thing.

Mass is the amount of matter or material in an object.

Weight is the measurement of the force of gravity on an object.

Many books use the word 'weight' to mean the same as 'mass'.

Metric units of mass are **grams** and **kilograms**.

There are 1000 grams in 1 kilogram.

1000 g = 1 kg
500 g = $\frac{1}{2}$ kg

Practice

1 Write how many grams are in each of these masses.

a $2\frac{1}{2}$ kg = ☐ g   b $3\frac{1}{4}$ kg = ☐ g   c $\frac{3}{4}$ kg = ☐ g

d 10.5 kg = ☐ g   e $2\frac{3}{4}$ kg = ☐ g   f 6.5 kg = ☐ g

2 Write these as kilograms and grams.

a 2400 g = ☐ kg ☐ g   b 1700 g = ☐ kg ☐ g   c 3550 g = ☐ kg ☐ g

d 5850 g = ☐ kg ☐ g   e 1020 g = ☐ kg ☐ g   f 4230 g = ☐ kg ☐ g

3 Write the weight of each parcel in kilograms and grams.

a    b 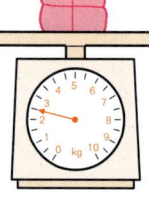   c 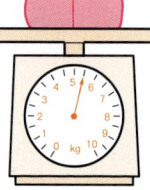   d 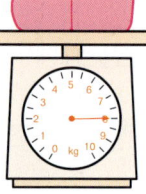   e   f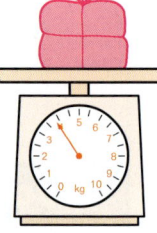

___kg _____g ___kg _____g ___kg _____g ___kg _____g ___kg _____g ___kg _____g

Challenge

4 Answer the problems.

a What is the total weight of parcels A and E? _____
b What is the difference in weight of parcels B and F? _____
c Which parcel is 750 g lighter than parcel C? _____
d How much heavier is parcel E than parcel B? _____
e How much lighter is parcel B than parcel C? _____
f Which two parcels have a total weight of $1\frac{1}{2}$ kg? _____

5 Round each weight to the nearest 100 g.

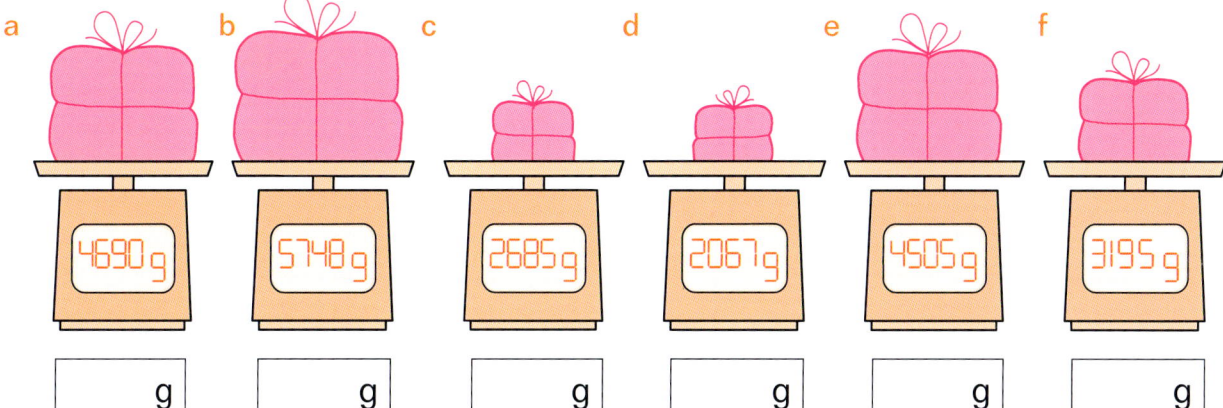

a 4690 g   b 5748 g   c 2685 g   d 2067 g   e 4505 g   f 3195 g

☐ g   ☐ g   ☐ g   ☐ g   ☐ g   ☐ g

Teacher's tips

As with any measurement problem, make sure all units are expressed the same before you start. With weight, don't be distracted by the size of the object. Bigger doesn't always mean heavier!

Topic 15: 3D shapes

Get started

3D means 3-dimensional and shows that it is a solid shape. Here are the names of some of these shapes.

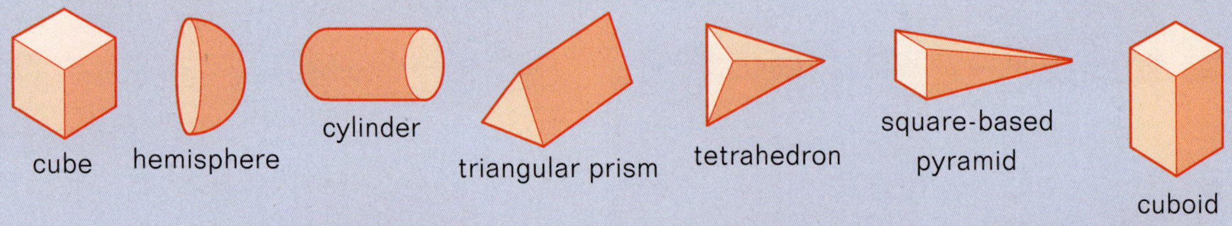

cube   hemisphere   cylinder   triangular prism   tetrahedron   square-based pyramid   cuboid

We can talk about how many faces, corners (vertices) and edges a 3D shape has.

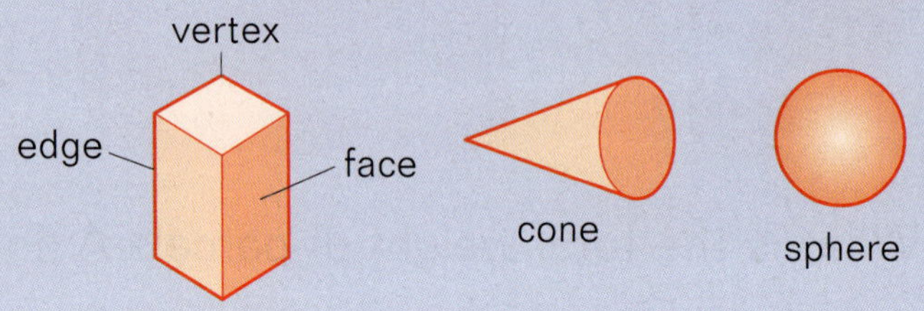

vertex, edge, face, cone, sphere

Practice

1. Name each shape.

   a _____   b _____   c _____   d _____   e _____   f _____

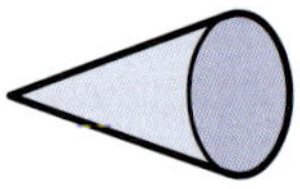

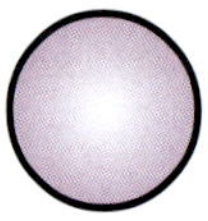

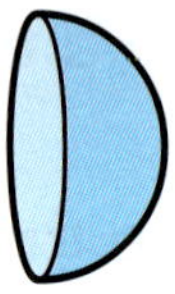

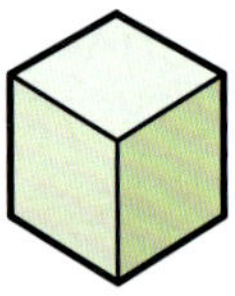

   g _____

2. Tick the odd shape out in each set.

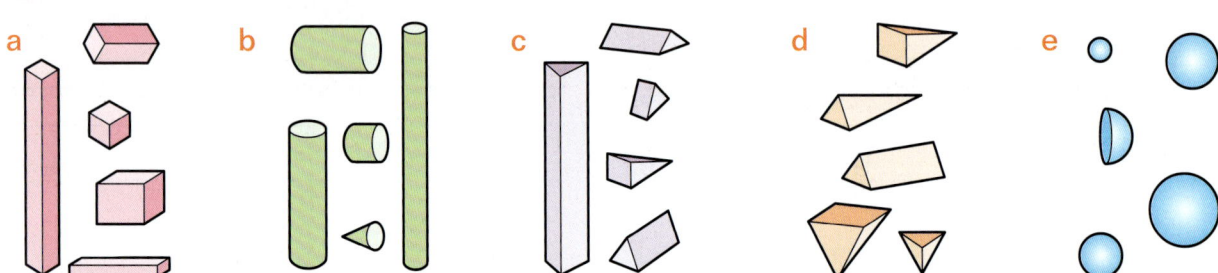

Challenge

3 How many faces are there in each of these 3D shapes?

a

____ square face and
____ triangular faces

b

____ triangular faces and
____ rectangular faces

c

____ square faces and
____ rectangular faces

d

____ triangular faces

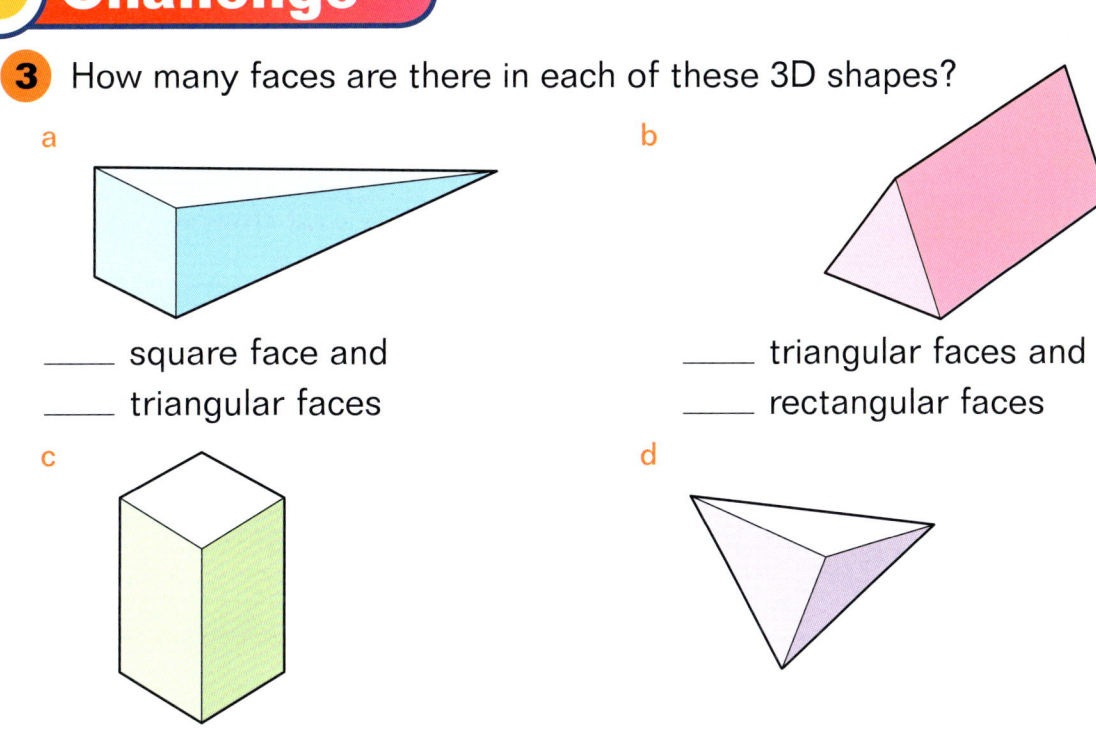

4 The name of each shape is muddled up. Try to work out each one from the clues.

a Six square faces – the shape of a dice.
BUCE _____

b Four triangular faces – a special pyramid.
TORNHEARTED _____

c Two square faces and four rectangular faces – the name for a box.
CODUBI _____

d A circular face and no point – half a marble.
SHEPHERIME _____

Teacher's tips

Think about the meaning of the prefixes when dealing with shapes, they always give a big clue! For instance 'tri' means 3, 'quad' means 4 and 'semi' means half.

Topic 16: Multiplication

Get started

Use your tables to multiply bigger numbers in your head.

Example

To multiply tens by a single digit, write the table fact and then make it ten times bigger: $70 \times 5 = 7 \times 5 \times 10 = 35 \times 10 = 350$

To multiply a 2-digit number by a single digit, break up the 2-digit number.

38×4

1. Multiply the tens: $30 \times 4 = 120$
2. Multiply the units: $8 \times 4 = 32$
3. Add the two parts: $120 + 32 = 152$

Practice

1 Write the answers.

a $20 \times 3 =$ ☐   b $60 \times 2 =$ ☐   c $40 \times 5 =$ ☐   d $70 \times 3 =$ ☐   e $30 \times 4 =$ ☐

f $50 \times 5 =$ ☐   g $90 \times 6 =$ ☐   h $30 \times 9 =$ ☐   i $80 \times 4 =$ ☐   j $70 \times 2 =$ ☐

k $30 \times 8 =$ ☐   l $20 \times 7 =$ ☐   m $80 \times 3 =$ ☐   n $40 \times 9 =$ ☐   o $60 \times 4 =$ ☐

2 Double each number.

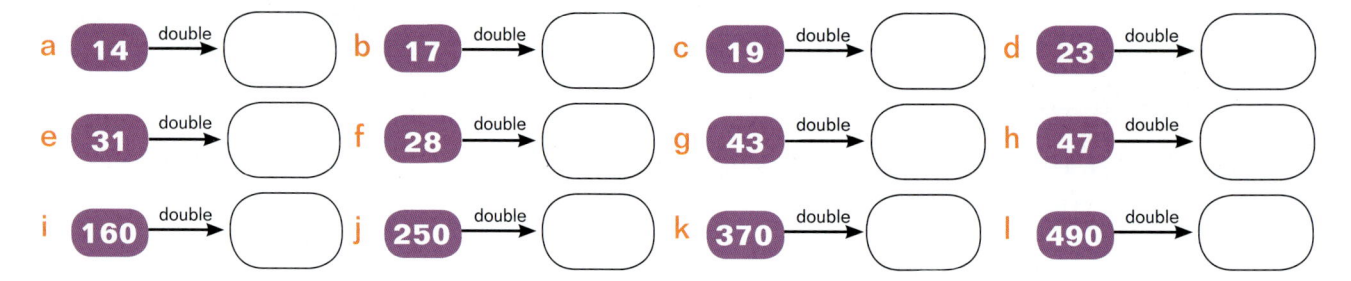

a 14 double ☐   b 17 double ☐   c 19 double ☐   d 23 double ☐

e 31 double ☐   f 28 double ☐   g 43 double ☐   h 47 double ☐

i 160 double ☐   j 250 double ☐   k 370 double ☐   l 490 double ☐

Teacher's tips

It's sometimes easy to forget that multiplication can be done in any order, so swap the problem round if it helps you to solve it. Try to break problems down into the times tables you know best.

Challenge

3 Answer these. Do them in your head.

a 45 × 4 = ☐ b 23 × 3 = ☐ c 37 × 5 = ☐ d 24 × 3 = ☐ e 42 × 5 = ☐
f 51 × 3 = ☐ g 63 × 5 = ☐ h 58 × 2 = ☐ i 64 × 4 = ☐ j 55 × 3 = ☐
k 69 × 4 = ☐ l 74 × 5 = ☐ m 86 × 2 = ☐ n 79 × 3 = ☐ o 88 × 4 = ☐

4 Answer these problems.

a What is 43 multiplied by 6? ☐
b There are 24 hours in a day. How many hours are there in a week? ☐
c Sam scored 49 points in a game. Jo scored double Sam's score. What did Jo score? ☐
d Apples are packed with 64 to each box. How many apples are there in five boxes? ☐
e A train ticket costs £38. What is the total cost for four tickets? ☐
f What number is double 99? ☐

5 Use the grids to answer these.

a 36 × 8

x	30	6
8	240	48

= 288

b 53 × 7

x	50	3
7		

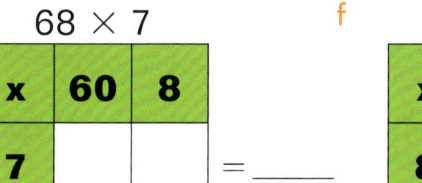

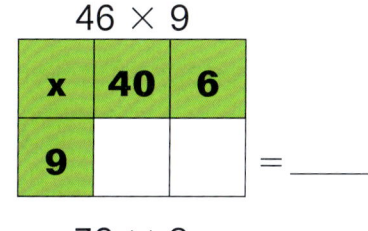

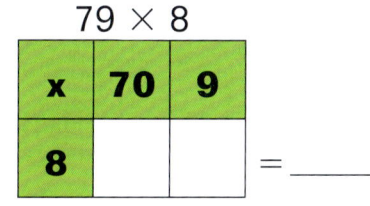

= ___

c 46 × 9

x	40	6
9		

= ___

d 78 × 6

x	70	8
6		

= ___

e 68 × 7

x	60	8
7		

= ___

f 79 × 8

x	70	9
8		

= ___

6 Write the missing digits 1 to 6 to complete these. Use each digit only once.

1 2 3 4 5 6

a 2◯ × 6 = ◯38   b ◯5 × 7 = 31◯   c ◯8 × 9 = 61◯

39

Topic 17: Division

Get started

Division is the inverse or opposite of multiplication.

So if you know your tables, it will help you to divide numbers.

$7 \times 3 = 21$

$21 \div 3 = 7$

$21 \div 7 = 3$

There are several ways of writing a division:

$30 \div 6$

$\frac{30}{6}$

$6 \overline{)30}$

All these mean 30 divided by 6.

Sometimes divisions aren't exact and leave **remainders**.

$20 \div 3 = 6$ remainder 2 or 6r2

Practice

1 Write the answers.

a $24 \div 3 =$ ☐   b $18 \div 2 =$ ☐   c $45 \div 5 =$ ☐   d $30 \div 3 =$ ☐   e $28 \div 4 =$ ☐

f $60 \div 5 =$ ☐   g $42 \div 6 =$ ☐   h $32 \div 2 =$ ☐   i $60 \div 4 =$ ☐   j $54 \div 3 =$ ☐

k $72 \div 3 =$ ☐   l $76 \div 4 =$ ☐   m $85 \div 5 =$ ☐   n $78 \div 6 =$ ☐   o $92 \div 4 =$ ☐

2 Halve each number.

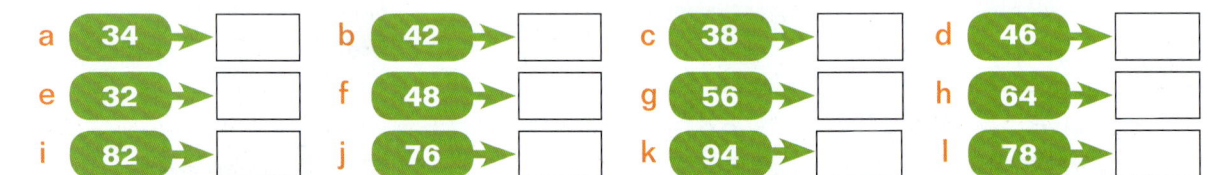

a 34 → ☐   b 42 → ☐   c 38 → ☐   d 46 → ☐

e 32 → ☐   f 48 → ☐   g 56 → ☐   h 64 → ☐

i 82 → ☐   j 76 → ☐   k 94 → ☐   l 78 → ☐

3 Answer these. Remember to include the remainder.

a $35 \div 4 =$ ☐ r ☐   b $26 \div 3 =$ ☐ r ☐   c $47 \div 2 =$ ☐ r ☐

d $44 \div 3 =$ ☐ r ☐   e $\frac{71}{3} =$ ☐ r ☐   f $\frac{83}{2} =$ ☐ r ☐

g $\frac{59}{4} =$ ☐ r ☐   h $\frac{74}{5} =$ ☐ r ☐   i $89 \div 6 =$ ☐ r ☐

Challenge

4 Answer these problems.

a What is 75 divided by 5? ☐

b What number is half of 98? ☐

c There are 54 children on a Cub outing.
   How many groups of six children can be made? ☐

d Toby spent 84p on 6 pencils. How much was each pencil? ☐

e I have 42 cakes. Each box holds 4 cakes. How many boxes will I need? ☐

f A magazine costs £3 each month. Jack has £38.
   How many magazines will he be able to get? ☐

5 Match each division to a remainder. Write a division for the spare remainder.

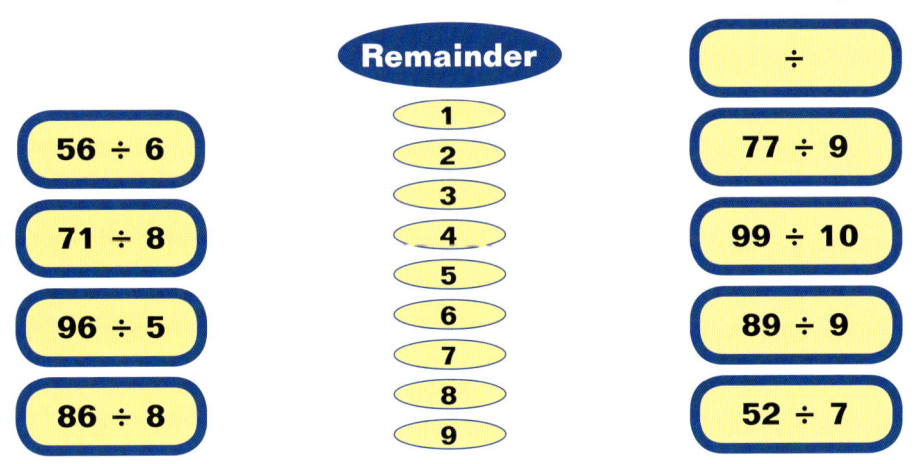

÷

Remainder
1
2
3
4
5
6
7
8
9

56 ÷ 6
71 ÷ 8
96 ÷ 5
86 ÷ 8

77 ÷ 9
99 ÷ 10
89 ÷ 9
52 ÷ 7

6 Write the missing digits 1 to 6 to complete these. Use each digit only once.

1 2 3 4 5 6

a 75 ÷ ◯ = 2◯   b 9◯ ÷ 2 = ◯6   c ◯2 ÷ 2 = ◯

Teacher's tips

When a Maths problem is written as a 'story', write the key information (values and actions) above the text or on another sheet as a number sequence. You can also cross out information that doesn't help you solve the problem.

Topic 18: Coordinates

Get started

Coordinates show the exact position of a point on a grid.

The coordinates of A are (2, 4)

The coordinates of B are (4, 2)

Read the **horizontal** coordinate first and then the **vertical** coordinate.

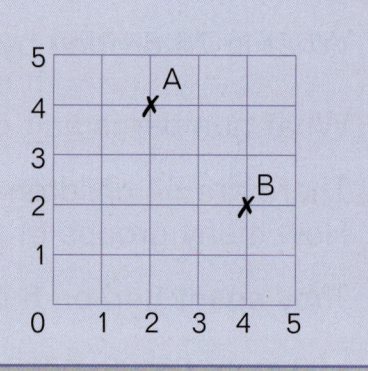

Practice

1 Look at these points and answer the questions.

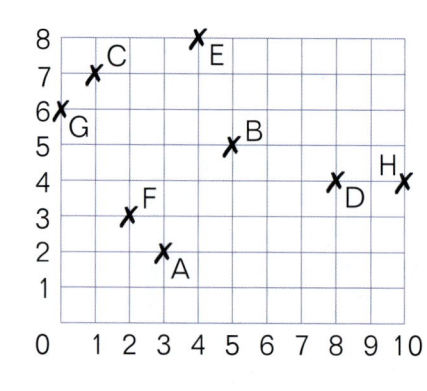

Write the coordinates of these points.

A → (___, ___)   F → (___, ___)

D → (___, ___)   H → (___, ___)

Write the letters for each of these points.

(5, 5) ☐   (0, 6) ☐   (4, 8) ☐   (1, 7) ☐

2 Plot and label these points on the grid.

A = (4, 1)   B = (6, 2)
C = (0, 1)   D = (5, 4)
E = (2, 0)   F = (8, 7)
G = (9, 3)   H = (7, 5)

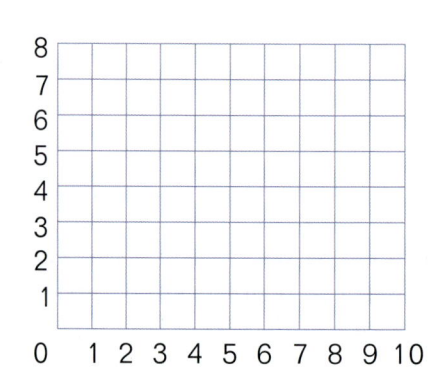

Challenge

3 Plot these points on the grid.

Use a ruler to join up the points in order to draw a shape.

A = (3, 4)   B = (4, 6)
C = (5, 4)   D = (7, 3)
E = (5, 2)   F = (4, 0)
G = (3, 2)   H = (1, 3)

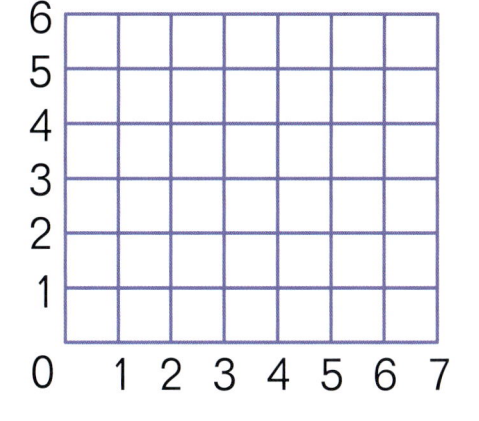

4 Design your own star on this grid.

Write the coordinates to show the position of each point.

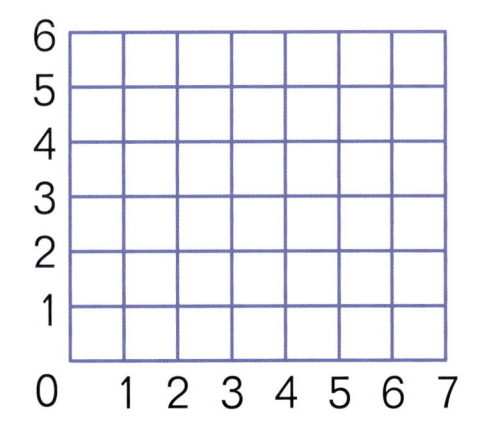

5 Here are three corners of a rectangle.

a What are the coordinates of the three corners?

A → (___,___) **B** → (___,___) **C** → (___,___)

b What would be the coordinates of the fourth corner, **D**? (___,___)

c Plot point **D** and complete the rectangle.

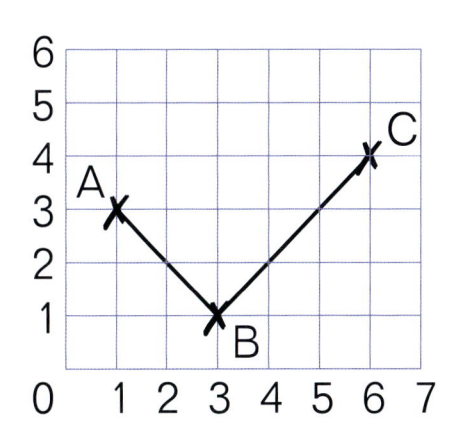

Teacher's tips

A good way to remember that you read coordinates horizontally and then vertically is simply that in the alphabet 'h' comes before 'v'!

43

Test 3: (Score 1 mark for every correct answer)

Topic 13

1 Round these to the nearest 10.

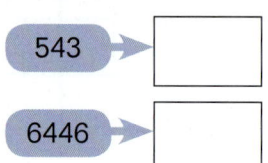

543 →

6446 →

2 Round these to the nearest 100.

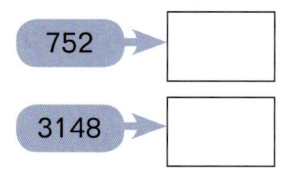

752 →

3148 →

3 Round these to the nearest pound.

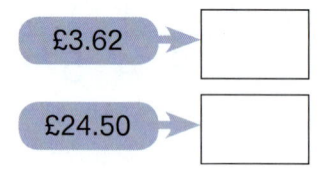

£3.62 →

£24.50 →

4 Estimate which tens number each arrow points to.

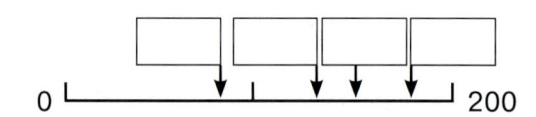

0 ⎯⎯⎯⎯⎯⎯⎯⎯⎯ 200

Topic 14

5 Write the missing amount.

$8\frac{1}{10}$ kg = ☐ g

6 Write this as kilograms and grams.

6225 g = ☐ kg ☐ g

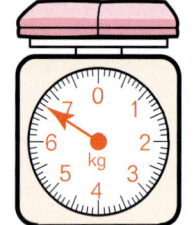

7 What is the weight of this parcel?

____ kg ____ g

8 What is the total weight of these two parcels?

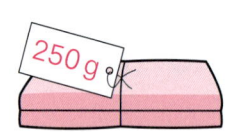

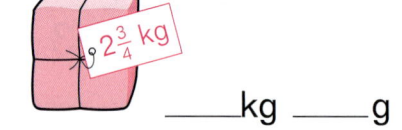

250 g $2\frac{3}{4}$ kg

____ kg ____ g

Topic 15

9 Name this shape.

_____

10 Tick the odd shape out.

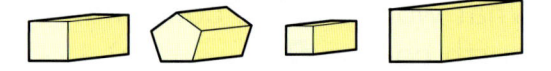

11 How many faces has this shape?

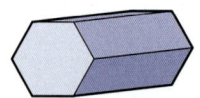

____ hexagonal faces

____ rectangular faces

12 Which shape has a square face and four triangular faces?

_____

44

Topic 16

13 Write the answer.

70 × 4 = ☐

14 What is double 56? ☐

15 Answer this mentally.

83 × 3 = ☐

16 Bulbs are packed in boxes of six. How many bulbs are there in 25 boxes? ☐

Topic 17

17 Write the answer.

64 ÷ 4 = ☐

18 What is half of 76? ☐

19 Answer this.

4)78 = ☐ r ☐

20 Callum has 81p. He buys five ice lollies and gets 1p change. How much does each ice lolly cost? ☐

Topic 18

Look at these points and answer the questions.

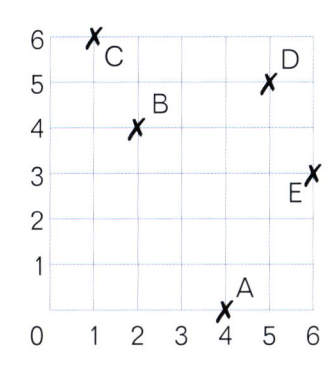

21 Write the coordinates for A (___,___)

22 Write the letter at position (1, 6) ☐

23 Write the coordinates for E (___,___)

24 Draw a cross at position (3, 5).

Mark the test. Remember to fill in your score on page 3.

Write your score out of 24. ☐

Add a bonus point if you scored 20 or more.

TOTAL SCORE FOR TEST 3 ☐

Topic 19: Decimals

Get started

A decimal point is used to separate whole numbers from fractions.

27.43
tens units tenths hundredths

$\frac{1}{10} = 0.1$ $\frac{1}{2} = 0.5$

$\frac{2}{10} = 0.2$ $\frac{1}{100} = 0.01$

Practice

1 Write these as decimals.

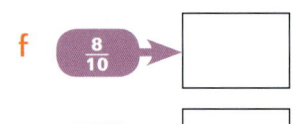

a $\frac{3}{10}$ → ☐   b $\frac{9}{10}$ → ☐   c $\frac{7}{10}$ → ☐   d $\frac{1}{2}$ → ☐

e $\frac{4}{10}$ → ☐   f $\frac{8}{10}$ → ☐   g $4\frac{1}{2}$ → ☐   h $2\frac{1}{10}$ → ☐

i $3\frac{7}{10}$ → ☐   j $5\frac{3}{10}$ → ☐   k $6\frac{9}{10}$ → ☐   l $4\frac{2}{10}$ → ☐

2 Write the decimals on these lines.

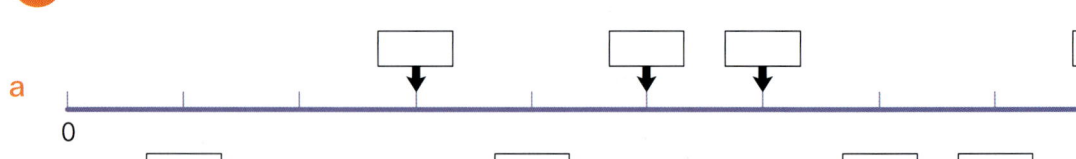

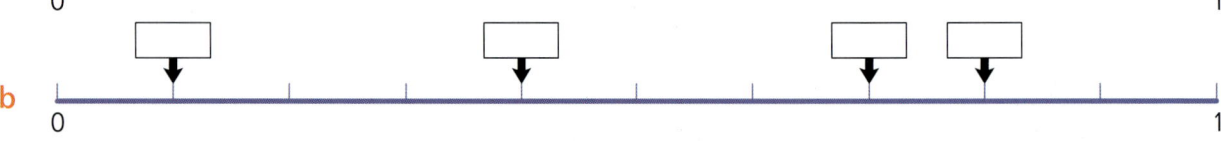

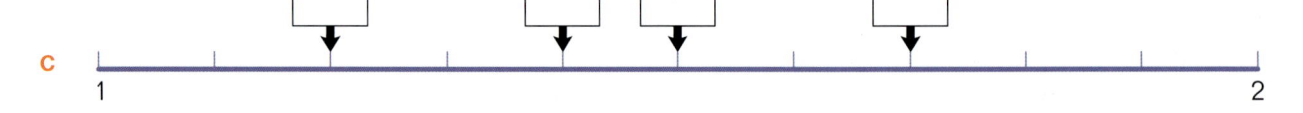

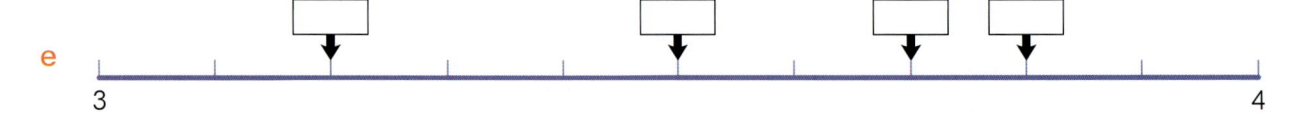

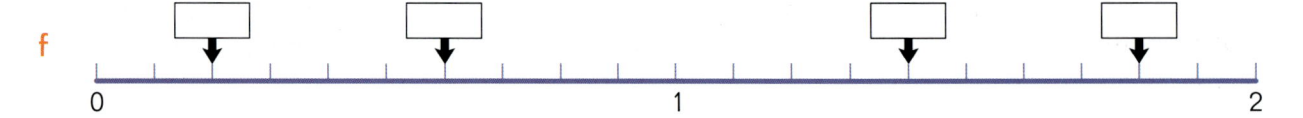

a 0 —————————————— 1

b 0 —————————————— 1

c 1 —————————————— 2

d 2 —————————————— 3

e 3 —————————————— 4

f 0 ————————— 1 ————————— 2

46

Challenge

3 Write the value of the bold digit as a fraction.

a 0.**3**5 ☐   b 6.**8** ☐   c 14.7**5** ☐   d 0.0**2** ☐   e 9.**3**6 ☐

f 8.0**7** ☐   g 15.**6**9 ☐   h 4.1**5** ☐   i 10.**8** ☐   j 16.**4**7 ☐

4 Put in the signs < or > so that these are true.

a 4.65 kg ☐ 4.70 kg   b 5.80 m ☐ 5.18 m   c £3.65 ☐ £3.56
d 3.25 ☐ 3.2   e 3.15 ☐ 3.5   f 6.05 ☐ 6.5
g 2.34 ☐ 2.43   h 8.66 ☐ 8.07

5 Write these numbers in order, starting with the smallest.

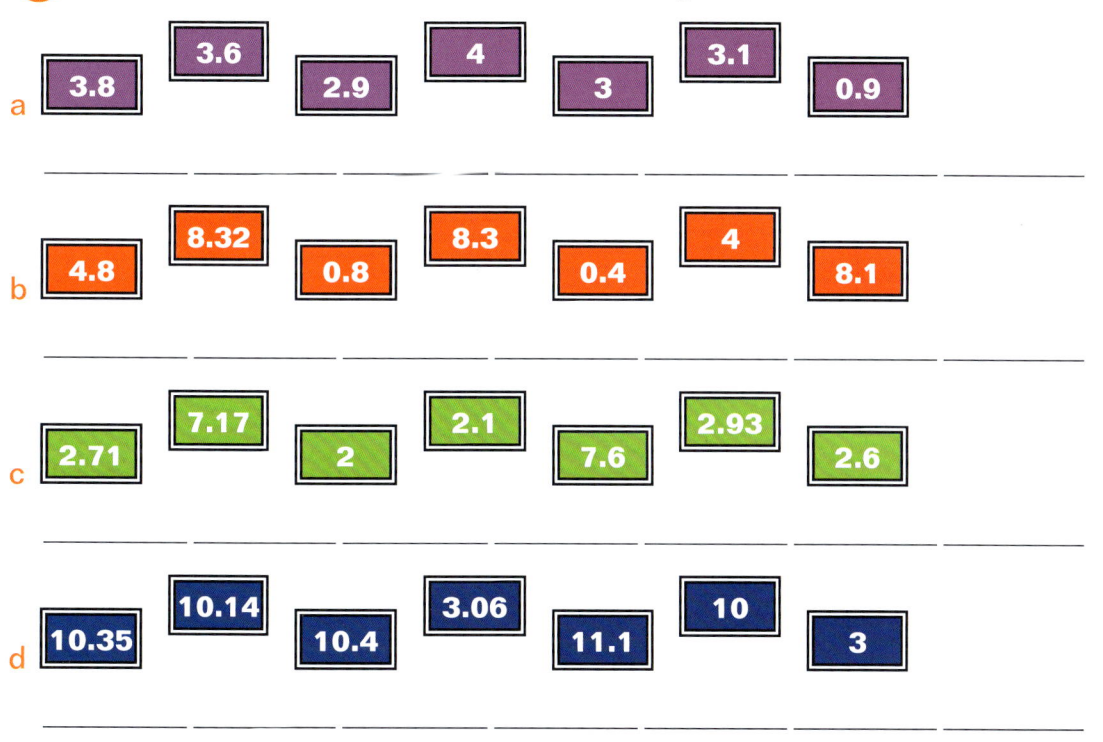

a 3.8 | 3.6 | 2.9 | 4 | 3 | 3.1 | 0.9

b 4.8 | 8.32 | 0.8 | 8.3 | 0.4 | 4 | 8.1

c 2.71 | 7.17 | 2 | 2.1 | 7.6 | 2.93 | 2.6

d 10.35 | 10.14 | 10.4 | 3.06 | 11.1 | 10 | 3

Teacher's tips

The **value** of a number is the same whether it is expressed as a fraction or a decimal. When comparing numbers it always helps to express them to the same number of decimal points, or as factors with the same denominator.

Topic 20: Capacity

Get started

Capacity is about how much something holds.

Metric units of capacity are litres and millilitres.

ml is short for millilitre.

l is short for litre.

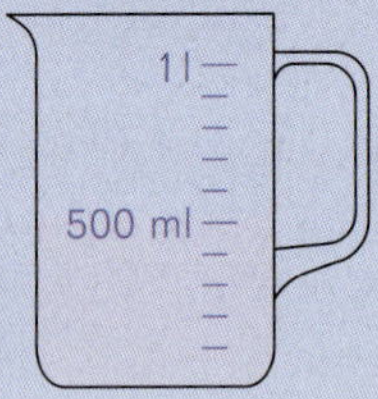

There are **1000 millilitres** in **1 litre**.

1000 ml = 1 l

500 ml = $\frac{1}{2}$ l

100 ml = $\frac{1}{10}$ l

Practice

1 Write how many millilitres are in each of these capacities.

a $1\frac{1}{2}$ l = ____ ml   b $2\frac{1}{4}$ l = ____ ml   c $\frac{1}{4}$ l = ____ ml   d $2\frac{1}{10}$ l = ____ ml

e 6.5 l = ____ ml   f $4\frac{3}{4}$ l = ____ ml   g 8.5 l = ____ ml   h $12\frac{3}{10}$ l = ____ ml

2 Write these as litres and millilitres.

a 4300 ml = ____ l _____ ml   b 1900 ml = ____ l _____ ml
c 6550 ml = ____ l _____ ml   d 2350 ml = ____ l _____ ml
e 2020 ml = ____ l _____ ml   f 6730 ml = ____ l _____ ml
g 4525 ml = ____ l _____ ml   h 1975 ml = ____ l _____ ml

3 Write the amount shown in each jug.

a _____ ml   b _____ ml   c _____ ml   d _____ ml   e _____ ml

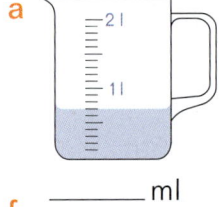

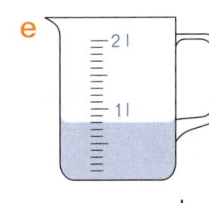

f _____ ml   g _____ ml   h _____ ml   i _____ ml   j _____ ml

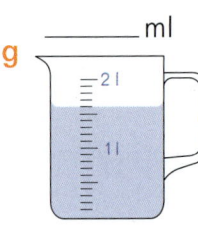

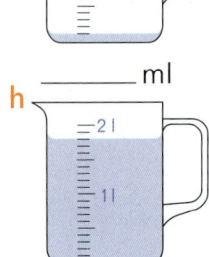

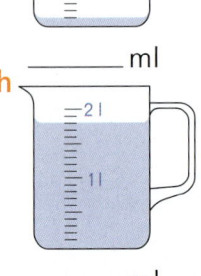

48

Challenge

4 Answer the problems.

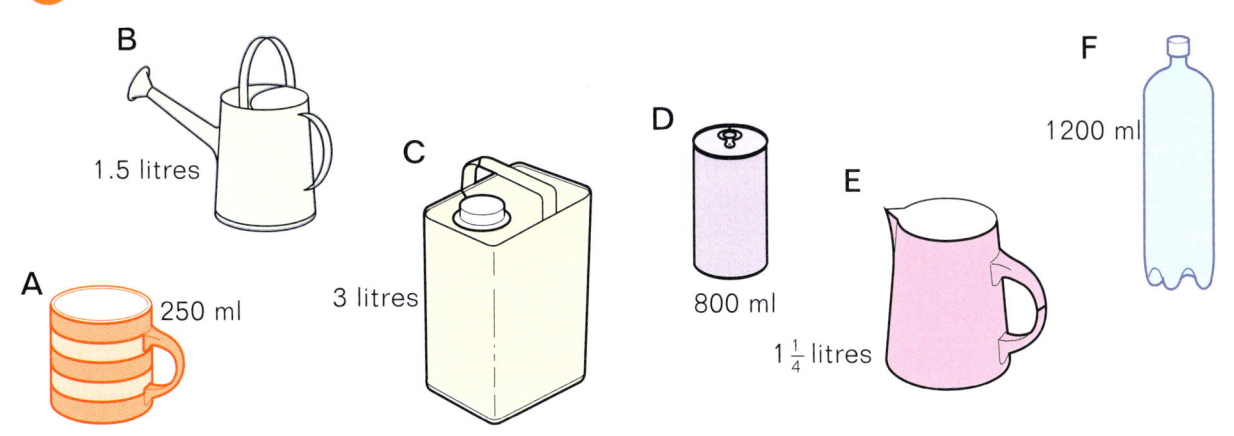

B — 1.5 litres
A — 250 ml
C — 3 litres
D — 800 ml
E — 1¼ litres
F — 1200 ml

a What is the total capacity of containers A and E?

b What is the difference in capacity of containers F and D?

c Which container has double the capacity of container B?

d How much more does container E hold than container F?

e How much less does container A hold than container D?

f Which two containers have a total capacity of 2 litres?

5 Round these to the nearest 100 ml.

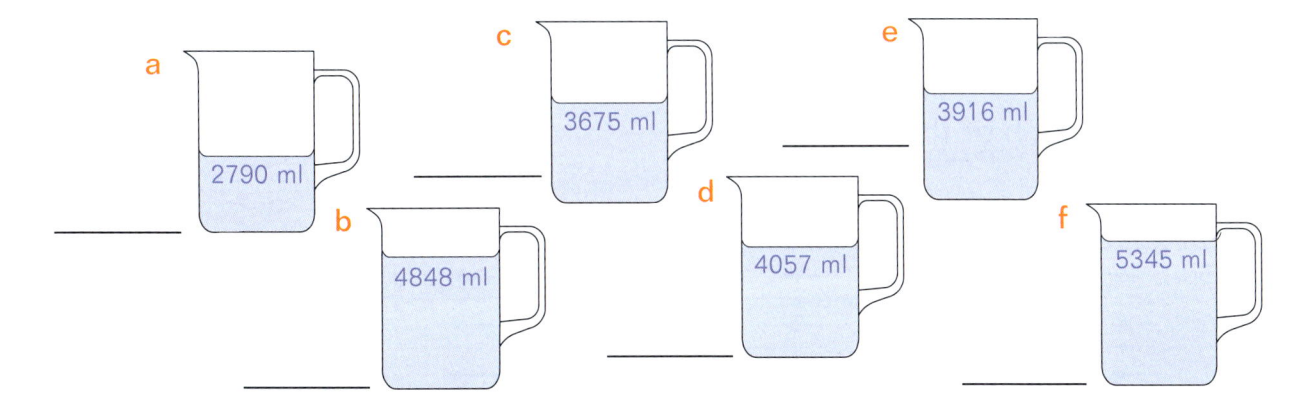

a 2790 ml
b 4848 ml
c 3675 ml
d 4057 ml
e 3916 ml
f 5345 ml

Teacher's tips

Use the table to convert from parts of a litre into millilitres. Convert the answer back into litres when you've solved the problem. Visualise a litre measuring jug being filled up with the different quantities to 'sense check' your answer.

Topic 21: Fractions of amounts

Get started

Fractions have a **numerator** and a **denominator**.

$\frac{1}{3}$ of 6 is the same as 6 ÷ 3 = 2

1 ← **numerator** (top number)
3 ← **denominator** (bottom number)

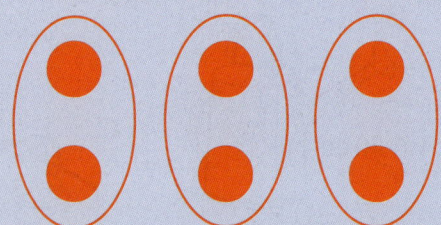

The denominator shows the number of equal parts.

The numerator shows the number of those parts you are dealing with.

Practice

1 Work out the fraction of each amount.

a Colour $\frac{1}{2}$ of the circles and write the answer.

○○○○○○ $\frac{1}{2}$ of 6 = ☐

○○○○○○○○○○ $\frac{1}{2}$ of 10 = ☐

○○○○○○○○ $\frac{1}{2}$ of 8 = ☐

○○○○○○○○○○○○ $\frac{1}{2}$ of 12 = ☐

b Colour $\frac{1}{4}$ of the circles and write the answer.

○○○○○○○○ $\frac{1}{4}$ of 8 = ☐

○○○○○○○○○○○○○○○○ $\frac{1}{4}$ of 16 = ☐

○○○○ $\frac{1}{4}$ of 4 = ☐

○○○○○○○○○○○○ $\frac{1}{4}$ of 12 = ☐

2 Answer each of these.

a $\frac{1}{3}$ of …

15	→
12	→
21	→
18	→
30	→

b $\frac{1}{5}$ of …

20	→
15	→
30	→
40	→
25	→

c $\frac{1}{4}$ of …

20	→
32	→
24	→
40	→
36	→

d $\frac{1}{10}$ of …

30	→
80	→
70	→
60	→
100	→

Challenge

3 Answer these.

1p 2p 5p 10p 20p 50p £1

a
What fraction of £1 is:
50p →
20p →
10p →
25p →
75p →

b
What fraction of £2 is:
20p →
£1 →
50p →
£1.50 →
40p →

c
What fraction of £10 is:
£2.50 →
£5 →
£1 →
£7.50 →
£2 →

4 Answer these.

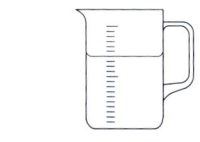

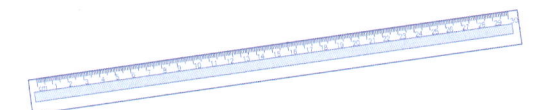

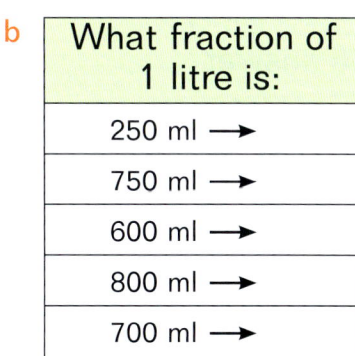

a
What fraction of 1 kilogram is:
100 g →
400 g →
200 g →
500 g →
300 g →

b
What fraction of 1 litre is:
250 ml →
750 ml →
600 ml →
800 ml →
700 ml →

c
What fraction of 1 metre is:
50 cm →
25 cm →
10 cm →
75 cm →
20 cm →

5 Colour this grid to make a pattern. Use these fractions for each colour.

$\frac{1}{4}$ red

$\frac{1}{6}$ blue

$\frac{1}{12}$ yellow

$\frac{1}{3}$ green

$\frac{1}{8}$ orange

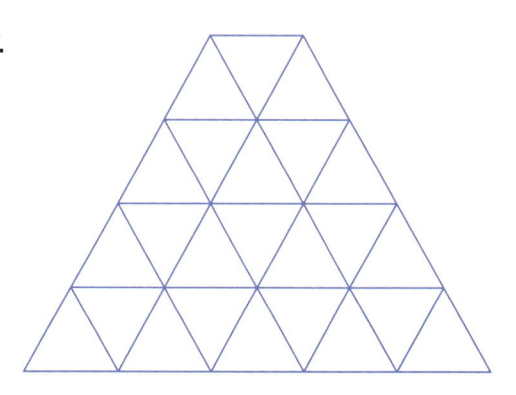

How many triangles are left white? _____

> **Teacher's tips**
>
> To work out fractions of amounts first convert quantities into the same units, then make the total amount (usually larger) the denominator, and the part you want to express as a fraction the numerator. Simplify the fraction.

51

Topic 22: Graphs

Get started

Pictograms are graphs that have pictures.

Each picture stands for a number. Look at the **key** to see how many each picture stands for.

Some graphs have **bars** or **columns**.

The axes have **labels** that give you information.

You must look carefully at the numbered axis to see what **scale** is being used.

The scale does not always go up in ones.

Practice

1 This pictogram shows the number of visitors to a museum in a week.

Look at the pictogram and answer these questions.

Key
🏠 represents 5 visitors
🏠 represents between 1 and 5 visitors

Days	
Mon	🏠🏠🏠🏠🏠🏠
Tues	🏠🏠🏠🏠🏠🏠
Wed	
Thurs	🏠🏠🏠🏠
Fri	🏠🏠🏠🏠🏠🏠
Sat	🏠🏠🏠🏠🏠🏠🏠🏠
Sun	🏠🏠🏠🏠🏠🏠

a How many visitors went to the museum on Tuesday? _____

b On which day did 37 people visit the museum? _____

c On which two days did the same number of people visit the museum?
_____

d Approximately how many people visited the museum on Thursday? ____

e On which two days were there fewer visitors than on Monday?
_____

f 14 of the visitors on Tuesday were children. How many adults were there on Tuesday? _____

g 88 people visited the museum at the weekend. How many visited on Saturday? _____

h Why do you think there were no visitors on Wednesday?
_____

52

Challenge

2 This bar chart shows the number of bikes sold each month by a bike shop.

Use the graph to answer these questions.

a How many bikes were sold in June? _____

b In which month were the most bikes sold? _____

c In which month were 56 bikes sold? _____

d How many bikes were sold in total in July and August? _____

e In which month were half the number of bikes sold compared to December? _____

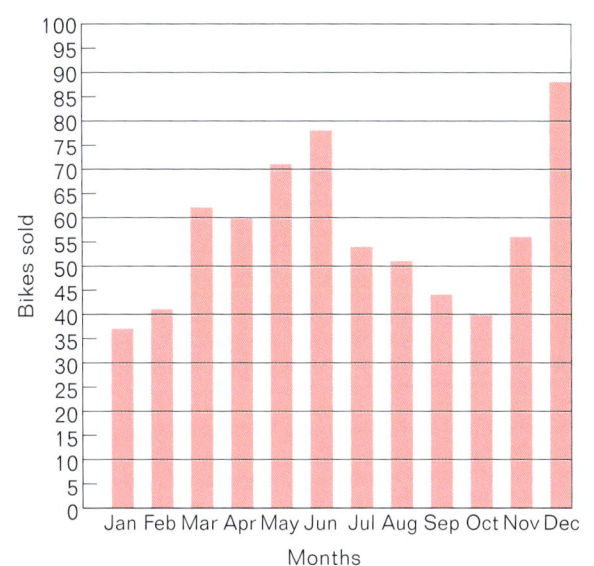

3 This table of results shows the times of six riders in a cycle race. Complete the graph and answer the questions.

Alan	Ben	Chris	David	Eric	Fred
48 mins	52 mins	39 mins	46 mins	43 mins	40 mins

a Who had the fastest time? _____

b Which cyclist finished six minutes behind Fred? _____

c Which cyclist finished nine minutes ahead of Ben? _____

d Write the cyclists in the order they finished.

1 _____ 2 _____
3 _____ 4 _____
5 _____ 6 _____

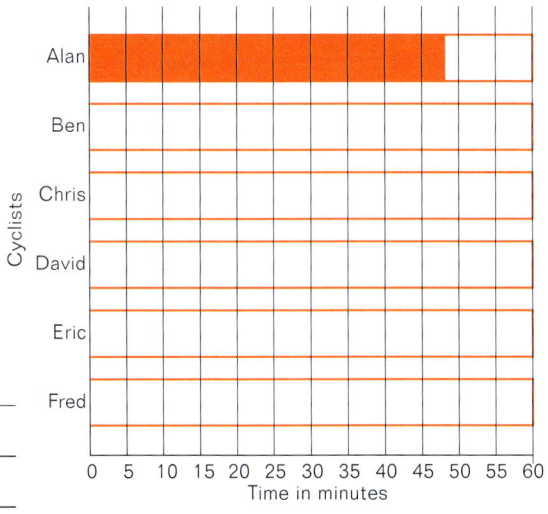

Teacher's tips

The most important things on any graph are the **labels** and the **scale**; make sure you read both very carefully before taking any readings.

Topic 23: Money

Get started

There are 100 pence in £1. When we write amounts as pounds and pence, we separate the pounds from the pence with a decimal point.

£1.40 = 140p   £3.09 = 309p
£5.38 = 538p   £0.85 = 85p

Practice

1 Write these totals.

a (20p, 5p, 10p, 5p) ____ p
b (1p, 2p, 20p, 50p) ____ p
c (10p, 20p, 1p, 2p) ____ p
d (5p, 5p, 5p, 5p) ____ p
e (10p, 1p, 20p, 50p) ____ p
f (20p, 50p, 10p, 10p) ____ p
g (1p, 5p, 50p, 1p) ____ p
h (10p, 20p, 20p, 20p) ____ p
i (2p, 2p, 50p, 20p) ____ p
j (10p, 1p, 2p, 50p) ____ p

2 Write these amounts in a different way.

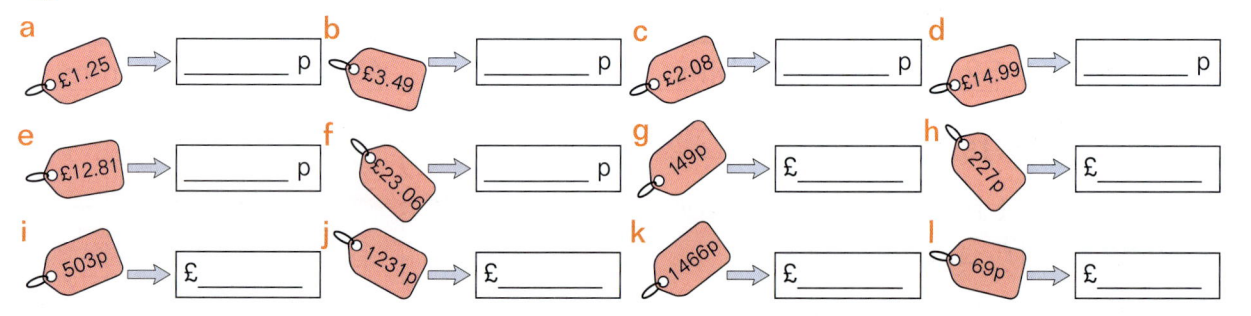

a £1.25 → ____ p
b £3.49 → ____ p
c £2.08 → ____ p
d £14.99 → ____ p
e £12.81 → ____ p
f £23.06 → ____ p
g 149p → £ ____
h 227p → £ ____
i 503p → £ ____
j 1231p → £ ____
k 1466p → £ ____
l 69p → £ ____

3 Write the change from each of these.

a **Change from £1**

48p →	85p →
37p →	64p →
91p →	29p →

b **Change from £5**

£4.30 →	£2.85 →
£3.21 →	£4.06 →
£2.97 →	£1.84 →

c **Change from £10**

£8.75 →	£9.22 →
£6.99 →	£4.83 →
£7.56 →	£8.47 →

Teacher's tips

When problems are expressed in words try writing them out as a number sentence to clarify how you're going to solve them. If there are 2 or more parts think carefully about which part you need to solve first.

Challenge

4 Answer these problems.

a Jo buys four pairs of socks at 80p a pair.
How much change does she get from £5? _____

b How many 8p sweets can David buy with 70p? _____

c What is the total cost of four stamps at 30p and six stamps at 42p? _____

d What is the change from £10 for six videos at £1.20 each? _____

e Doughnuts cost £1.09 a pack. What is the cost of three packs? _____

f CDs cost £7.49 in the sales. What change from
£20 will there be for two CDs? _____

5 Answer these.

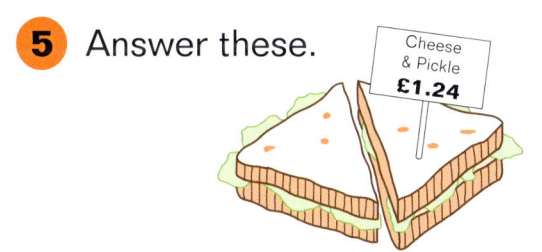

Cheese & Pickle **£1.24**

Sausage roll **63p** each

Samosa **38p** each

a How much will three sausage rolls cost? _____

b What is the total cost of a cheese and pickle sandwich and
two sausage rolls? _____

c How much will ten samosas cost? _____

d What is the change from £5 for two cheese and pickle sandwiches
and a samosa? _____

6 A magazine costs £1.28.

The smallest number of coins needed to pay for
it exactly is 5.

1p 2p 5p 20p £1

£1.28 MAGAZINE OF THE MONTH

a Write four other amounts that need exactly 5 of
any coins.

_____

b Write four amounts that need exactly 6 of any coins.

_____

c What is the lowest amount that you can make with 6 different coins? ☐

Topic 24: Angles

Get started

Angles are measures of turn. They are measured in **degrees**.

- A complete turn is 360°
- Half a complete turn is 180°. This looks like a straight line
- A quarter turn is 90°, also called a right angle.
- The three angles of an equilateral triangle are 60° each.
- Half a right angle is 45°.

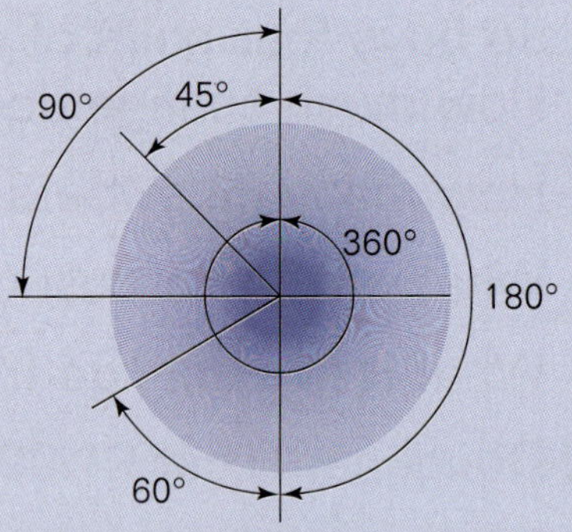

There are 8 compass directions:

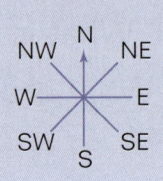

North, North-east, East, South-east, South, South-west, West, North-west

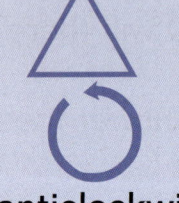

clockwise   anticlockwise

Practice

1 These angles show either 360°, 180°, 90°, 60° or 45°.

Write the size of each angle.

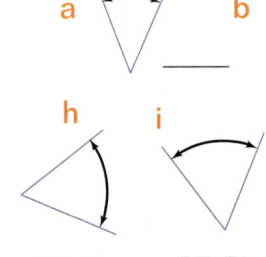

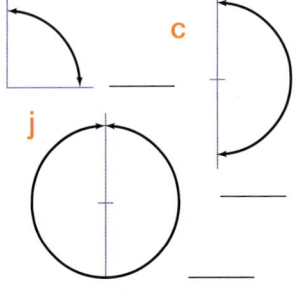

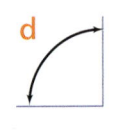

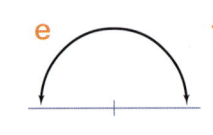

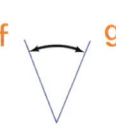

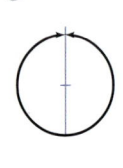

a   b   c

d   e   f   g

h   i   j

2 Write where you will face after each turn: N, S, E or W.

Face North to start each time
a Turn 180° clockwise. ___
b Turn 90° anticlockwise. ___
c Turn 45° clockwise. ___

Face East to start each time
g Make 360° turn anticlockwise. ___
h Make 90° turn clockwise. ___
i Make 45° turn anticlockwise. ___

Face South to start each time
d Turn 90° anticlockwise. ___
e Turn 45° clockwise. ___
f Turn 180° clockwise. ___

Face West to start each time
j Make 180° turn clockwise. ___
k Make 45° turn clockwise. ___
l Make 90° turn anticlockwise. ___

Challenge

3 Tick the right angles on these shapes.

How many right angles are there altogether? _____

4 Write these angles in order of size, starting with the smallest.

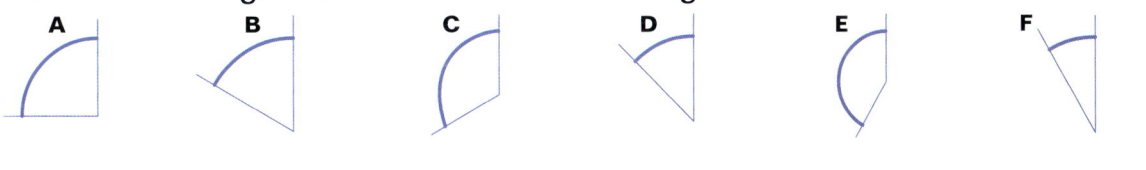

A   B   C   D   E   F

_____ _____ _____ _____ _____ _____

5 Look at this dial from a washing machine.

The arrow turns clockwise. Answer these questions.

a How many degrees does the arrow turn from:
pre-wash to spin _____
wash to rinse _____
rinse to off _____
pre-wash to dry _____

b Write the position the arrow is pointing to after these turns:
60° from pre-wash _____
120° from spin _____
180° from wash _____
360° from off _____

Teacher's tips

To remember the order of North, South, East, West use an abbreviation like 'Never Eat Soggy Waffles', or make your own up.

Test 4: (Score 1 mark for every correct answer)

Topic 19

1 Write these as decimals.

$\frac{3}{10}$ = ☐ $\frac{1}{2}$ = ☐

2 Write the decimals on this line.

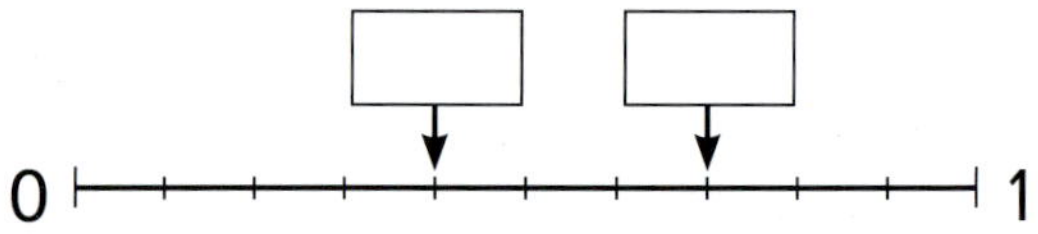

0 ├──────────────┤ 1

3 What is the value of the digit 5 in this number?

12.57 ☐

4 Write the correct signs < or > for these.

4.6 ☐ 4.8 ☐ 4.3

Topic 20

5 Write the missing amount.

$3\frac{1}{10}$ litres = _____ ml

6 Write this as litres and millilitres.

4805 ml = ___ l _____ ml

7 How much liquid is in this jug?

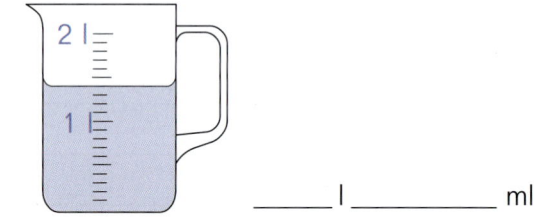

___ l _____ ml

8 What is the difference between these two amounts? _____

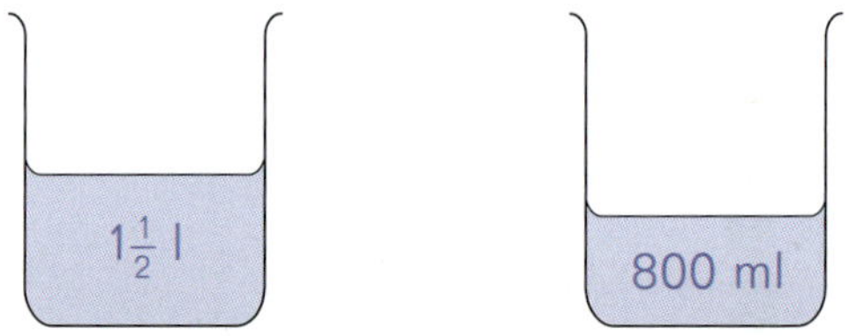

$1\frac{1}{2}$ l   800 ml

Topic 21

9 Circle $\frac{1}{3}$ of the stars and write the answer.

$\frac{1}{3}$ of 12 = ☐

10 What is one-fifth of 30? ____

11 What fraction of £2 is 50p? ☐

12 What fraction of 1 kilogram is 750 g? ☐

Topic 22

This bar chart shows a survey of the pets owned by a group of people.

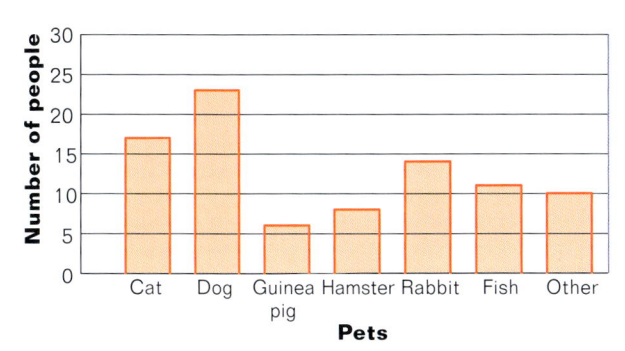

13 How many people had a dog? _____

14 Which pet was owned by 14 people? _____

15 How many more people owned a cat than a fish? _____

16 How many guinea pigs and hamsters were there altogether? _____

Topic 23

17 Write the total.

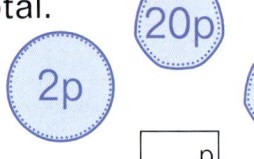

20p 2p 50p 5p

☐ p

18 Write these amounts.

£3.76 = _____ p

1245p = £_____

19 A T-shirt costs £6.89. What change would be given from £10? ☐

20 Harry bought six felt-pens for 96p. How much would two felt-pens cost? ☐

Topic 24

21 Write the size of this angle. _____°

22 Tick the right angles on this shape. ☐

23 If you face North and turn anticlockwise by 45°, which direction will you now be facing? _____

24 Tick the angle that shows 60°.

Mark the test. Now add up all your test scores and put your final score on page 3.

Write your score out of 24. ☐

Add a bonus point if you scored 20 or more.

TOTAL SCORE FOR TEST 4 ☐

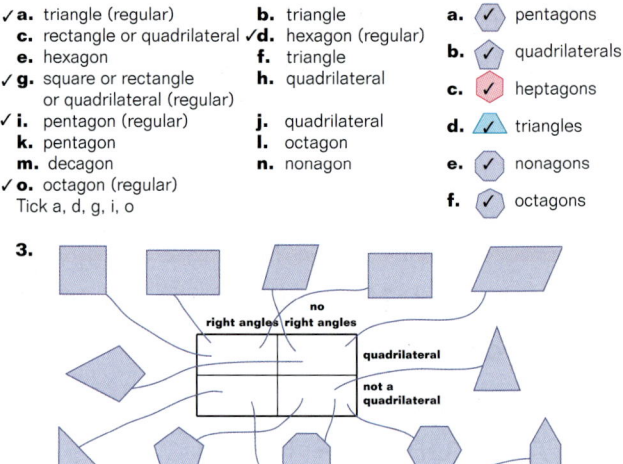

Answers

Topic 1: Place value (page 4)

1.
a. 2100 b. 9184
c. 1480 d. 6206
e. 5680 f. 4935
g. 8057 h. 6092
i. 3001 j. 1009

2.
a. 600
b. 100 + 40 + 5
c. 3000 + 200 + 90 + 8   d. 6000
f. 9000 + 800 + 30 + 4
g. 400 + 90
h. 500 + 90 + 8
i. 4000 + 600 + 80 + 9   j. 7000 + 90 + 4
k. 5000 + 800 + 90   l. 2000 + 900 + 40 + 6

(Note: 2. e. 9000 + 300 + 7)

3.
a. 3099, 3248, 4769, 4796, 4966
b. 3080, 3445, 3546, 3550, 4992
c. 6009, 6097, 6109, 6977, 7102
d. 4020, 4200, 4399, 4559, 4560
e. 8090, 8329, 8392, 8900, 8932
f. 5002, 5020, 5022, 5202, 5222

4.
a. 40 b. 2000 c. 6000
d. 600 e. 80 000 f. 50 000
g. 40 000 h. 50 i. 6000
j. 90 k. 10 000 l. 20

5. Any 10 of these numbers:
3489 3498 3849 3894 3948 3984
4389 4398 4839 4893 4938 4983
8349 8394 8439 8493 8934 8943
9348 9384 9438 9483 9834 9843

Topic 2: Addition facts (page 6)

1.
a. 11 b. 14 c. 19 d. 20
   10   14   19   19
   14   10   25   28
   11   13   16   21
   16   12   21   23
   12   17   25   22
   11   10   22   23
   18   11   18   23

2.
a. 60
b. 40
c. 70
d. 30
e. 80
f. 50
g. 20
h. 90
i. 10

3.
a. 110   b. 130
   120   110
   130   150
   120   140
c. 800   d. 800
   1300   1100
   1100   1100
   1500   1300

4.
a. 14 b. 17 c. 16
   24   27   26
   34   37   36
   44   47   46
   54   57   56
d. 15 e. 13
   25   23
   35   33
   45   43
   55   53

5.
a. 15 b. 1100
c. 90 d. 25
e. 21 f. 900
g. 100 h. 27
i. 61 j. 41
k. 170 l. 27
m. 26 n. 34

6.
a.
IN   4 7 9 16 13 15 18 23
OUT 13 16 18 25 22 24 27 32
b.
IN   4 8 1 7 13 11 7 14
OUT 23 27 20 26 32 30 26 33

Topic 3: Subtraction facts (page 8)

1.
a. 11 b. 10 c. 16 d. 28
   7   6   23   28
   7   9   17   28
   8   9   17   25
   11   9   17   32
   15   9   21   28
   8   5   18   24
   6   14   21   29
   13   8   16   29
   8   8   18   29

2.
a. 50 b. 130
   30   70
   30   40
   10   80
   40   120
c. 300 d. 1500
   400   1100
   500   1100
   300   300
   300   700

3.
a. 5 b. 6 c. 3 d. 6
   9   8   8   9
   7   8   10   5
   8   10   6   7
  10   13   14   15
   4   15   17   12

4.
a. 8 b. 50
c. 5 d. 30
e. 8 f. 70
g. 8 h. 40
i. 7 j. 400
k. 11 l. 500

5.
a. 20, 6
b. 80, 10, 4
c. 75, 60, 15
d. 95, 40, 5

Topic 4: Length (page 10)

1.
a. 5 km b. 10 km c. 3.5 km
d. 0.5 km e. 6000 m f. 20 m
g. 7500 m h. 5.25 m i. 2 m
j. 70 mm k. 6.5 m l. 635 cm
m. 4 cm n. 1200 m o. 1.5 cm

2.
a. 6 cm
   4 cm
   5 cm
   3 cm
b. 4.5 cm, 45 mm
   2.5 cm, 25 mm
   6.5 cm, 65 mm
   5.5 cm, 55 mm

3.
a. 55 mm
b. 47 mm
c. 64 mm
d. 37 mm

4.
a. 35 cm
b. 9 km
c. 5.5 km
d. 1 m 60 cm
e. 700 cm
f. 230 km

5.
a. 3 cm
b. 12 cm
c. 4.5 cm
d. 13.5 cm
e. 8 cm
f. 5 cm

Topic 5: Multiplication and division facts (page 12)

1.
a. 5 × 7 = 35   7 × 5 = 35   35 ÷ 5 = 7   35 ÷ 7 = 5
b. 9 × 4 = 36   4 × 9 = 36   36 ÷ 9 = 4   36 ÷ 4 = 9
c. 6 × 3 = 18   3 × 6 = 18   18 ÷ 6 = 3   18 ÷ 3 = 6
d. 5 × 6 = 30   6 × 5 = 30   30 ÷ 5 = 6   30 ÷ 6 = 5
e. 9 × 3 = 27   3 × 9 = 27   27 ÷ 9 = 3   27 ÷ 3 = 9
f. 7 × 6 = 42   6 × 7 = 42   42 ÷ 7 = 6   42 ÷ 6 = 7
g. 8 × 9 = 72   9 × 8 = 72   72 ÷ 9 = 8   72 ÷ 8 = 9

2.
a. 45 b. 18 c. 7 d. 6
   24   42   3   4
   64   20   5   7
   27   32   5   4
   24   49   3   7
   24   21   6   2
   30   40   9   4

3.
a. IN   4 3 7 9 5 8
   OUT 24 18 42 54 30 48
b. IN 1 5 6 2 7 9 4
   OUT 45 54 18 63 81 36 (values as shown)
c. IN 28 12 36 32 16 20
   OUT 7 3 9 8 4 5
d. IN 18 21 27 15 12 24
   OUT 6 7 9 5 4 8

4.
a.
x	6	8	4
3	18	24	12
9	54	72	36
2	12	16	8

b.
x	4	9	3
8	32	72	24
7	28	63	21
5	20	45	15

c.
x	4	6	7
2	8	12	14
5	20	30	35
8	32	48	56

d.
x	4	5	8
2	8	10	16
3	12	15	24
6	24	30	48

e.
x	3	7	9
4	12	28	36
7	21	49	63
8	24	56	72

f.
x	4	6	10
3	12	18	30
5	20	30	50
10	40	60	100

Topic 6: 2D shapes (page 14)

1.
✓a. triangle (regular)   b. triangle
c. rectangle or quadrilateral   ✓d. hexagon (regular)
e. hexagon   f. triangle
✓g. square or rectangle   h. quadrilateral
   or quadrilateral (regular)
✓i. pentagon (regular)   j. quadrilateral
k. pentagon   l. octagon
m. decagon   n. nonagon
✓o. octagon (regular)
Tick a, d, g, i, o

2.
a. pentagons
b. quadrilaterals
c. heptagons
d. triangles
e. ✓ nonagons
f. ✓ octagons

3. (Sorting diagram: right angles / no right angles × quadrilateral / not a quadrilateral)

60

Test 1: (page 16)

1. 6047
2. 7000 + 200
3. 6047, 6704, 6740, 7064, 7604
4. 60,000
5. 14, 24, 34
6. 8
7. 120
8. 20
9. 13
10. 70
11. 16
12. 900
13. 8 cm, 6.5 km
14. 1.5 cm, 15 mm
15. 6.5 cm or 65 mm
16. 8 cm
17. 8 × 4 = 32   4 × 8 = 32   32 ÷ 4 = 8   32 ÷ 8 = 4
18. 42, 8
19. IN   4 7 6 9 8 2
    OUT 32 56 48 72 64 16
20.

x	3	8	7
4	12	32	28
6	18	48	42
9	27	72	63

21. pentagons ✓
22. rectangle and quadrilateral
23. The pentagon is the odd one out; all the others are hexagons.
24. The two bottom corners are right angles.

Topic 7: Time (page 18)

1.
a. 7:20
b. 4:15
c. 6:55
d. 10:40
e. 8:17
f. 12:37
g. 5:03
h. 9:29

2. a. b. c. d.

3.
Church Street	8.50 a.m.	9.35 a.m.	11.00 a.m.	1.05 p.m.
Marsh Lane	9.15 a.m.	10.00 a.m.	11.25 a.m.	1.30 p.m.
Hospital	9.40 a.m.	10.25 a.m.	11.50 a.m.	1.55 p.m.
Swimming pool	10.05 a.m.	10.50 a.m.	12.15 p.m.	2.20 p.m.

4.
a. 8.05 p.m.
b. 1 hour and 25 minutes
c. 1.15 p.m.
d. 1.25 p.m.
e. 6 hours and 5 minutes

5.
a. 20 minutes slow
b. 40 minutes slow
c. 4 minutes slow
d. 16 minutes slow
e. 55 minutes slow
f. 36 minutes slow

Topic 8: Fractions of shapes (page 20)

1.
a. $\frac{1}{4}$
b. $\frac{1}{3}$
c. $\frac{1}{8}$
d. $\frac{1}{5}$
e. $\frac{1}{10}$
f. $\frac{1}{6}$
g. $\frac{2}{5}$
h. $\frac{3}{4}$
i. $\frac{3}{8}$
j. $\frac{4}{5}$
k. $\frac{9}{10}$
l. $\frac{4}{5}$

2.
a. $\frac{1}{3} = \frac{2}{6}$
b. $\frac{1}{2} = \frac{6}{12}$
c. $\frac{1}{5} = \frac{3}{15}$
d. $\frac{1}{4} = \frac{4}{16}$
e. $\frac{1}{2} = \frac{5}{10}$
f. $\frac{1}{4} = \frac{3}{12}$

3.
a. $\frac{1}{3}$
b. $\frac{3}{4}$
c. $\frac{1}{2}$
d. $\frac{1}{5}$
e. $\frac{3}{5}$
f. $\frac{1}{4}$

4.
a. Any 3 boxes should be shaded.
b. Any 2 boxes should be shaded.
c. Any 4 boxes should be shaded.
d. Any 4 boxes should be shaded.
e. Any 2 boxes should be shaded.
f. Any 3 boxes should be shaded.

5. $\frac{1}{12}$ $\frac{1}{6}$ $\frac{1}{4}$ $\frac{1}{3}$ $\frac{2}{5}$ $\frac{3}{4}$ $\frac{5}{6}$

Topic 9: Addition (page 22)

1.
a. 110   b. 85   c. 60
d. 120   e. 115   f. 90
g. 130   h. 125   i. 100
j. 100   k. 105   l. 130

2.
a. 95   b. 115   c. 123   d. 98
e. 157   f. 76   g. 88   h. 79
i. 90   j. 89   k. 92   l. 82
m. 91   n. 91   o. 81   p. 126
q. 147   r. 131   s. 141   t. 142

3.
a.
53	47	100
28	31	59
81	78	159

b.
31	67	98
42	39	81
73	106	179

c.
62	57	119
38	29	67
100	86	186

d.
62	53	115
74	47	121
136	100	236

4.
74 → 37
68 → 43
67 → 44
47 → 64
78 → 33
57 → 54

5.
a. 28 + 67 = 95
b. 59 + 74 = 133
c. 81 + 64 = 145

Topic 10: Subtraction (page 24)

1.
a. 38   b. 37
c. 24   d. 24
e. 17   f. 28
g. 26   h. 29
i. 17   j. 35

2.
a. 21   b. 33   c. 22   d. 44
e. 34   f. 34   g. 27   h. 47
i. 38   j. 55   k. 36   l. 17
m. 25   n. 27   o. 38   p. 37
q. 27   r. 39   s. 25   t. 26

3.
a. 18   b. 16   c. 9   d. 16
e. 28   f. 17   g. 16   h. 25

4.
83 → 39
62 → 18
93 → 49
52 → 96
33 → 77
53 → 97

5.
a. 83 − 57 = 26   b. 94 − 68 = 26   c. 74 − 48 = 26

Topic 11: Sequences and patterns (page 26)

1.
a. 15   b. 27   c. 125   d. 270   e. 65
   17   32   127   280   60
   19   37   129   290   55
f. 500   g. 26   h. 18   i. 43   j. 160
   400   29   22   40   150
   300   32   26   37   140

2.
a. 24   b. 83   c. 410   d. 38   e. 99
   30   58   460   46   101
   36   53   710   50   109
f. 120   g. 82   h. 89   i. 47   j. 710
   125   46   73   62   510
   135   28   69   65   310

3.
a. −5, −4, 1, 2
b. −25, −20, 5, 10
c. −6, −5, 0, 1
d. −18, −15, 0, 3
e. −14, −12, −2, 0
f. −10, −7, 8, 11
g. −11, −9, 1, 3
h. −18, −14, 6, 10

4.
a. 35, 30
b. 31, 27
c. 43, 49
d. 468, 476
e. 910, 940
f. 144, 148

5.
1	2	3	4	5	6	7	8
9	10	11	12	13	14	15	16
17	18	19	20	21	22	23	24
25	26	27	28	29	30	31	32
33	34	35	36	37	38	39	40
41	42	43	44	45	46	47	48
49	50	51	52	53	54	55	56
57	58	59	60	61	62	63	64

Topic 12: Comparing and ordering numbers (p28)

1.
a. 306, 368, 380, 800, 806, 860
b. 405, 450, 486, 589, 590, 594
c. 659, 689, 690, 906, 965, 966
d. 205, 215, 505, 512, 520, 522
e. 2599, 3005, 3125, 3152, 3502
f. 1670, 1706, 5799, 7509, 7611
g. 8079, 8095, 8307, 8345, 8543
h. 7244, 7323, 7324, 7332, 7342

2.
a. < b. < c. >
d. > e. > f. <
g. > h. > i. <

3.
a. 685 b. 4050
c. 530 d. 5690
e. 860 f. 1060
g. 390 h. 6475
i. 720 j. 8340

4.
a. < > b. > >
c. < < d. > <
e. < > f. > >

5.
Island	Area (sq km)
Great Britain	218 041
Iceland	103 000
Ireland	83 766
Sicily	25 400
Sardinia	23 800
Cyprus	9251
Corsica	8270
Crete	8260

Test 2 (page 30)

1. 6.12
2. [clock showing time]
3. 50 minutes
4. 9.00
5. $\frac{3}{5}$
6. $\frac{1}{4} = \frac{2}{8}$
7. $\frac{1}{8}$
8. Any six boxes should be shaded
9. 165
10. 152
11.
53	47	**100**
28	31	**59**
81	**78**	**159**
12. 67 and 58
13. 38
14. 28
15. 45 and 93
16. 72 − 46 = 26
17. 28 and 33
18. 52 and 34
19. −14, −11, 4, 7
20. 37 and 41
21. 4679, 4767, 4769, 4799
22. 6105 < 6150
    4355 > 4335
23. 4220
24. 6104 > 3259 < 3260

Topic 13: Rounding numbers (page 32)

1.
a. 460 b. 280
c. 150 d. 310
e. 640 f. 840
g. 1470 h. 9280

2.
a. 700 b. 500
c. 100 d. 600
e. 800 f. 900
g. 4900 h. 7800

3.
a. £1 b. £5
c. £2 d. £6
e. £5 f. £9
g. £13 h. £16

4. These are estimates.
a. 20 50 70 90
b. 50 80 150 250
c. 60 90 130 180
d. 120 200 400 480

5. These are estimates.
a. 200 400 700 900
b. 600 800 2300 2700
c. 500 900 1400 1800
d. 800 1900 3300 4700

6. These are estimates.
a. 380 b. 5900
   740   9600
   170   2600
   410   3300
   600   80 000
   1000   200 000

Topic 14: Weight and mass (page 34)

1.
a. 2500 g
b. 3250 g
c. 750 g
d. 10 500 g
e. 2750 g
f. 6500 g

2.
a. 2 kg 400 g
b. 1 kg 700 g
c. 3 kg 550 g
d. 5 kg 850 g
e. 1 kg 20 g
f. 4 kg 230 g

3.
a. 3 kg 500 g
b. 2 kg 500 g
c. 5 kg 500 g
d. 8 kg
e. 9 kg 600 g
f. 3 kg 900 g

4.
a. 2 kg
b. 300 g
c. E
d. 50 g
e. 800 g
f. D and F

5.
a. 4700 g
b. 5700 g
c. 2700 g
d. 2100 g
e. 4500 g
f. 3200 g

Topic 15: 3D shapes (page 36)

1.
a. cone
b. tetrahedron
c. sphere
d. hemisphere
e. cube
f. square-based pyramid
g. cylinder

2.
a. Cube – all the others are cuboids
b. Cone – all the others are cylinders
c. Square-based pyramid – all the others are prisms
d. Prism – all the others are pyramids
e. Hemisphere – all the others are spheres

3.
a. 1 square face and 4 triangular faces
b. 2 triangular faces and 3 rectangular faces
c. 2 square faces and 4 rectangular faces
d. 4 triangular faces

4.
a. cube
b. tetrahedron
c. cuboid
d. hemisphere

Topic 16: Multiplication (page 38)

1.
a. 60 b. 120
c. 200 d. 210
e. 120 f. 250
g. 540 h. 270
i. 320 j. 140
k. 240 l. 140
m. 240 n. 360
o. 240

2.
a. 28 b. 34
c. 38 d. 46
e. 62 f. 56
g. 86 h. 94
i. 320 j. 500
k. 740 l. 980

3.
a. 180 b. 69
c. 185 d. 72
e. 210 f. 153
g. 315 h. 116
i. 256 j. 165
k. 276 l. 370
m. 172 n. 237
o. 352

4.
a. 258
b. 168
c. 98
d. 320
e. £152
f. 198

5.
a. 288
b. 371
c. 414
d. 468
e. 476
f. 632

6.
a. 23 × 6 = 138
b. 45 × 7 = 315
c. 68 × 9 = 612

Topic 17: Division (page 40)

1.
a. 8 b. 9 c. 9 d. 10 e. 7
f. 12 g. 7 h. 16 i. 15 j. 18
k. 24 l. 19 m. 17 n. 13 o. 23

2.
a. 17 b. 21 c. 19 d. 23
e. 16 f. 24 g. 28 h. 32
i. 41 j. 38 k. 47 l. 39

3.
a. 8 r 3 b. 8 r 2 c. 23 r 1
d. 14 r 2 e. 23 r 2 f. 41 r 1
g. 14 r 3 h. 14 r 4 i. 14 r 5

4.
a. 15
b. 49
c. 9
d. 14p
e. 11
f. 12

5.
56 ÷ 6 → 2
71 ÷ 8 → 7
96 ÷ 5 → 1
86 ÷ 8 → 6
77 ÷ 9 → 5
99 ÷ 10 → 9
89 ÷ 9 → 8
52 ÷ 7 → 3

Check that the remainder for the child's own division is 4.

6.
a. 75 ÷ 3 = 25
b. 92 ÷ 2 = 46
c. 12 ÷ 2 = 6

Topic 18: Coordinates (page 42)

1.
A = (3, 2) F = (2, 3) D = (8, 4) H = (10, 4)
(5, 5) = B (0, 6) = G (4, 8) = E (1, 7) = C

2. Check coordinates are plotted correctly.

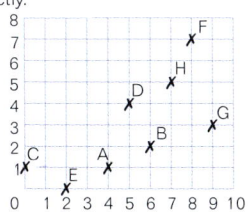

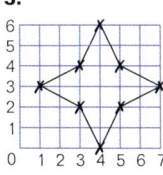

3. (grid with star shape)

4. Check child's coordinates are correct for the star drawn.

5.
a. A = (1, 3)
   B = (3, 1)
   C = (6, 4)
b. D = (4, 6)
c. Check corner D has been drawn in correctly at (4, 6).

Test 3 (page 44)

1. 540, 6450
2. 800, 3100
3. £4, £25
4. 80, 130, 150, 180 (these are estimates)
5. 8100 g
6. 6 kg 225 g
7. 6 kg 700 g
8. 3 kg 0 g
9. hemisphere
10. The odd one out is the pentagonal prism; all the others are cuboids.
11. 2 hexagonal faces and 6 rectangular faces
12. square-based pyramid
13. 280
14. 112
15. 249
16. 150
17. 16
18. 38
19. 19 r 2
20. 16p
21. (4, 0)
22. C
23. (6, 3)
24. Check the child's cross is correctly placed at (3, 5).

Topic 19: Decimals (page 46)

1.
a. 0.3 b. 0.9 c. 0.7 d. 0.5
e. 0.4 f. 0.8 g. 4.5 h. 2.1
i. 3.7 j. 5.3 k. 6.9 l. 4.2

2.
a. 0.3, 0.5, 0.6, 0.9
b. 0.1, 0.4, 0.7, 0.8
c. 1.2, 1.4, 1.5, 1.7
d. 2.1, 2.3, 2.6, 2.9
e. 3.2, 3.5, 3.7, 3.8
f. 0.2, 0.6, 1.4, 1.8

3.
a. $\frac{3}{10}$ b. $\frac{8}{10}$ c. $\frac{5}{100}$ d. $\frac{2}{100}$ e. $\frac{3}{10}$
f. $\frac{7}{100}$ g. $\frac{6}{10}$ h. $\frac{5}{100}$ i. $\frac{8}{10}$ j. $\frac{4}{10}$

4.
a. <
b. >
c. >
d. >
e. <
f. <
g. <
h. >

5.
a. 0.9, 2.9, 3, 3.1, 3.6, 3.8, 4
b. 0.4, 0.8, 4, 4.8, 8.1, 8.3, 8.32
c. 2, 2.1, 2.6, 2.71, 2.93, 7.17, 7.6
d. 3, 3.06, 10, 10.14, 10.35, 10.4, 11.1

Topic 20: Capacity (page 48)

1.
a. 1500 ml b. 2250 ml c. 250 ml d. 2100 ml
e. 6500 ml f. 4750 ml g. 8500 ml h. 12 300 ml

2.
a. 4 l 300 ml b. 1 l 900 ml c. 6 l 550 ml d. 2 l 350 ml
e. 2 l 20 ml f. 6 l 730 ml g. 4 l 525 ml h. 1 l 975 ml

3.
a. 700 ml b. 400 ml c. 100 ml d. 900 ml e. 800 ml
f. 1200 ml g. 1600 ml h. 1800 ml i. 1500 ml j. 1300 ml

4.
a. 1.5 l or 1$\frac{1}{2}$ l
b. 400 ml
c. C
d. 50 ml
e. 550 ml
f. F and D

5.
a. 2800 ml
b. 4800 ml
c. 3700 ml
d. 4100 ml
e. 3900 ml
f. 5300 ml

Topic 21: Fractions of amounts (page 50)

1.
a. 3
   5
   4
   6

b. 2
   4
   1
   3

2.
a. 5 b. 4 c. 5 d. 3
   4   3   8   8
   7   6   6   7
   6   8   10   6
         5   9   10

3.
a. $\frac{1}{2}$ b. $\frac{1}{10}$ c. $\frac{1}{4}$
   $\frac{1}{5}$ $\frac{1}{2}$ $\frac{1}{2}$
   $\frac{1}{10}$ $\frac{1}{4}$ $\frac{1}{10}$
   $\frac{1}{4}$ $\frac{3}{4}$ $\frac{3}{4}$
   $\frac{3}{4}$ $\frac{1}{5}$ $\frac{1}{5}$

4.
a. $\frac{1}{10}$ b. $\frac{1}{4}$ c. $\frac{1}{2}$
   $\frac{4}{10}$ or $\frac{2}{5}$ $\frac{3}{4}$ $\frac{1}{4}$
   $\frac{2}{10}$ or $\frac{1}{5}$ $\frac{6}{10}$ or $\frac{3}{5}$ $\frac{1}{10}$
   $\frac{1}{2}$ $\frac{8}{10}$ or $\frac{4}{5}$ $\frac{3}{4}$
   $\frac{3}{10}$ $\frac{7}{10}$ $\frac{2}{10}$ or $\frac{1}{5}$

5. Check that the triangles coloured are as follows
6 triangles red
4 triangles blue
2 triangles yellow
8 triangles green
3 triangles orange
1 triangle will be left white

Topic 22: Graphs (page 52)

1.
a. 40
b. Friday
c. Tuesday and Sunday
d. 16–19
e. Wednesday and Thursday
f. 26
g. 48
h. The museum was probably closed.

2.
a. 78
b. December
c. November
d. 105
e. September

3.
Check that the graph has been completed correctly.
a. Chris
b. David
c. Eric
d. Chris, Fred, Eric, David, Alan, Ben

Topic 23: Money (page 54)

1.
a. 40p b. 73p c. 33p d. 20p
e. 81p f. 90p g. 57p h. 70p
i. 74p j. 72p

2.
a. 125p b. 349p c. 208p d. 1499p
e. 1281p f. 2306p g. £1.49 h. £2.27
i. £5.03 j. £12.31 k. £14.66 l. £0.69

3.
a. 52p, 15p, 63p, 36p, 9p, 71p
b. 70p, £2.15, £1.79, 94p, £2.03, £3.16
c. £1.25, 78p, £3.01, £5.17, £2.44, £1.53

4.
a. £1.80
b. 8
c. £3.72
d. £2.80
e. £3.27
f. £5.02

5.
a. £1.89
b. £2.50
c. £3.80
d. £2.14

6.
a. Check which 5 coins add to each of the four amounts.
b. Check which 6 coins add to each of the four amounts.
c. Lowest possible amount with 6 different coins is
88p → 1p + 2p + 5p + 10p + 20p + 50p coins

Topic 24: Angles (page 56)

1.
a. 45° b. 90°
c. 180° d. 90°
e. 180° f. 45°
g. 360° h. 60°
i. 60° j. 360°

2.
a. S b. W
c. NE d. E
e. SW f. N
g. E h. S
i. NE j. E
k. NW l. S

3.
There are 16 right angles altogether.

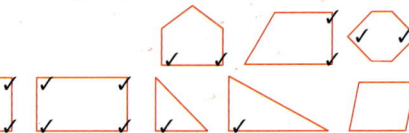

4.
F, D, B, A, C, E

5.
a. 180° b. WASH
60° OFF
180° DRY
240° OFF

Test 4 (page 58)

1. 0.3, 0.5
2. 0.4, 0.7
3. $\frac{5}{10}$
4. 4.6 < 4.8 > 4.3
5. 3100 ml
6. 4 l 805 ml
7. 1 l 400 ml
8. 700 ml
9. 4
10. 6
11. $\frac{1}{4}$
12. $\frac{3}{4}$
13. 23
14. rabbit
15. 6
16. 14
17. 77p
18. 376p, £12.45
19. £3.11
20. 32p
21. 180°
22. All four corners should be ticked on the rectangle.
23. NW
24.